Babycare
week by week

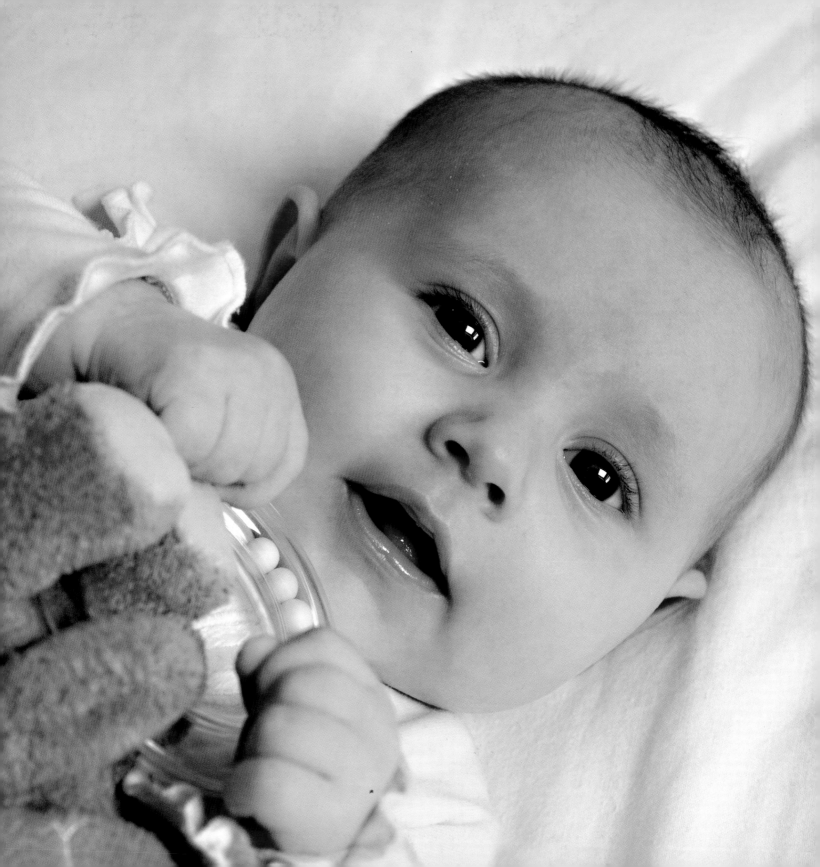

Babycare
week by week:
the first six months

Alison Mackonochie

Collins

To my husband Robin, with my
love and thanks for his unfailing
support over the years.

Alison Mackonochie has written
extensively on parenting issues. Having edited
a number of parenting magazines including
You & Your Baby, *Parents* and *Everything You
Need To Know About Your Baby*, she went on
to create and write *Emma's Diary*, the Royal
College of General Practitioners' hugely
successful pregnancy guide. Currently Editor-
in-Chief of *Emma's Diary*, Alison also writes
for magazines and newspapers and is the
author of numerous books on pregnancy
and childcare. She is a member of the
Medical Journalists' Association and the Guild
of Health Writers. Married with three children,
Alison lives and works in Bedfordshire.

The information contained in this
book is not intended nor implied to be
a substitute for professional medical
advice, and is provided for general
information and educational purposes
only. The author and the publishers
are not responsible or liable for any
medical diagnosis made by a reader
of this book based on its content.
Always seek professional advice from
your doctor or any other qualified
healthcare professional if you are in
any way concerned about the health
of your child.

First published in 2007 by Collins, an imprint of HarperCollins Publishers Ltd
77–85 Fulham Palace Road
London
W6 8JB

www.collins.co.uk
Collins is a registered trademark of HarperCollins Publishers Ltd.

Text © Alison Mackonochie 2007

8 7 6 5 4 3 2
11 10 09 08 07

A catalogue record for this book is available from the British Library.

ISBN-10: 0-00-724020-1
ISBN-13: 978-0-00-724020-3

Collins uses papers that are natural, renewable and recyclable products made
from wood grown in sustainable forests. The manufacturing processes
conform to the environmental regulations of the country of origin.

Designed by: Martin Hendry
Edited by: Diana Vowles

Printed in Singapore by Imago
Colour origination by Dot Gradations Limited, UK

Contents

Introduction

As a mum of three children – a boy and two girls – I know how crazy, even scary, those first weeks at home with a new baby can be. Suddenly your life is not your own any more; you're at the beck and call of a tiny, demanding infant who, without trying, has you wound round his or her little finger.

My children are now well past the baby stage, but I can still remember the elation and exhaustion of those early months, along with the need for reassurance and help when things didn't go as I expected. This support is what I hope this book will give you, especially if you are feeling rather alone and scared by the responsibility of having become a parent.

People often take it for granted that everyone knows how to look after a baby. But in reality, why should you know unless you've had younger siblings or close family with young babies? If you've had no previous experience it can all be a bit daunting. Try to remember that one day soon feeding, changing and bathing will have become familiar daily routines, but until then I hope the special baby know-how features in this book will help you cope.

It's wonderful watching your baby develop over these early weeks and months, but it's easy to become concerned if your baby isn't progressing as quickly as others you know. The pages on your baby's progress take you through the first 26 weeks of a baby's development – but do remember that every child is an individual who will develop at his or her own pace, so these sections should only be used as a general guide. Always talk to your doctor or health visitor if you have any concerns.

Becoming a parent isn't just about looking after your baby. There are many practical issues to be considered as well – things that you may never have given any thought to before now, such as how to register a baby's birth, paternity leave, baby bonds, making a will – the list goes on. This is why I've included a parents' survival guide which looks at some of the things you may need to consider as the weeks go by.

Your baby will be a baby for such a short period of time, and you'll find that these early weeks simply fly by. During this time I hope this book will be the 'friend' that you can turn to when you're unsure or want advice and that it will help you to enjoy every second of this very special time.

Your newborn baby

First appearances

A newborn's appearance can come as a surprise to first-time parents, as the baby very often doesn't look anything like the cherubic infant they probably imagined. But when you consider that your baby has spent nine months curled up in your uterus floating in amniotic fluid, then an average of twelve hours squeezing her way down the birth canal, it's unsurprising that she looks wrinkled and misshapen.

The first thing you may notice is that your baby's head looks too big for her body and rather cone-shaped. This is because, at birth, the head is around one-quarter of your baby's total length and it has been compressed and moulded as it passed down the birth canal. It will gain a normal

shape within a few days. If your baby had an assisted delivery there may also be bruising to her scalp from forceps or a soft tissue swelling (caput) caused by the suction from a ventouse extraction. These, too, will disappear in a few days.

You may be slightly alarmed at the soft pulsating spots that you can see on the top of your baby's head. These are the gaps where the skull bones haven't fused and are called fontanelles. Although they look delicate they are well protected by skin and fibrous tissue. Fontanelles close up gradually as your baby's head grows and by the time she is around 18 months they will have disappeared completely.

It's quite natural for your baby to appear 'scrunched up' and bow-legged. Her arms and legs have been confined by the lack of space in the uterus during the last weeks of pregnancy and it will take a little while for them to become uncurled. It's also likely that your baby's features will have been slightly flattened during delivery.

The umbilical cord will have been clamped and cut shortly after the birth, leaving a small stump attached to your

baby. Within a few hours the cord stump turns black as it dries out. It will drop off by itself, but until it does it will need to be treated with care.

Skin

Be prepared for your baby's skin to have a greyish-blue tinge; until the oxygen from her lungs has reached her bloodstream, her legs may even be a different colour from the rest of her body. She may have patches of dry skin and of vernix, the greasy white substance which has been protecting her skin from becoming waterlogged by the fluid she's been floating in. Some babies are born with a covering of fine hair called lanugo on their shoulders, upper arms and legs. All these features will gradually disappear.

Transient hormonal effects

Your baby's genitals may be enlarged and breasts slightly swollen – there may even be a slight milky discharge. This is caused by an increase in female hormones from the placenta just before birth and affects both boys and girls. Any swelling and discharge will soon disappear. Baby girls can even bleed slightly from the vagina, and both boys and girls can have breast

Weight and length

How much a baby weighs at birth can vary considerably, but the average weight is around 3.4 kg (7½ lb). The average length of a newborn is 48–51 cm (19–20 in), with your baby's likely length being somewhere between 45 cm (18 in) and 56 cm (22 in).

Parents' survival guide

Mums

You may be feeling on top of the world, physically, mentally and emotionally, or you may feel bruised, battered and exhausted. Most probably, you will be experiencing something between these two extremes. This is completely normal. The important thing right now is to be kind to yourself and your body and to allow yourself time to recover, both in body and spirit. Most importantly, enjoy every moment of this special time with your new baby.

Dads

Some men feel like fathers from the moment they see their child for the first time while, for others, it takes longer. If you are feeling rather detached from everything and a bit in awe of your new baby, don't worry; it's quite natural to feel this way, especially as the attention is now firmly on mum and child, leaving you out on a limb. You just need a bit of time to get to know your baby, so try adopting a hands-on approach so you can get to know her as you change, bath or rock her to sleep.

'buds' – small firm swellings behind one or both nipples. Once again this is a transient hormonal effect.

Hair and eyes

Your baby may be bald, or she may have a full head of hair. This will gradually drop out and be replaced with new hair over the next few months. This fresh growth can often be a completely different colour and texture to your baby's first hair.

Many babies are born with dark blue eyes, but this is likely to change over the course of the next few weeks or months. Exposure to the light changes the initial colour of the irises and a gradual increase in melanin, the body's natural pigmentation, means that your baby's eye colour may go on changing until she's around a year old. You can't always predict your baby's eye colour as it could be different from that of both her parents.

First milestones

Your newborn...

- can focus on objects that are within 20–30 cm (8–12 in), while objects that are further away are blurred
- hears and responds to noise
- can grip your finger tightly
- will suck vigorously
- may make walking movements when held on a hard surface
- will turn towards you when you stroke her cheek.

You...

- are likely to be feeling very tired, but elated
- will enjoy skin-to-skin contact with your baby
- will be encouraged to put your baby to the breast
- need to spend time alone with your partner and your new baby, so you can begin to bond as a family.

Caring for your newborn

First feeds

Your baby doesn't require a lot of nourishment during the first few days. This means that the small amount of colostrum your breasts produce after the birth is the ideal first food. You should put your baby to the breast whenever she seems hungry (*see* pp.22–3). It may take her a while to get used to feeding so you will need to be patient. Feeding on demand, especially during the first few days, will help your milk supply to increase. If you are bottle feeding, your baby will probably require no more than 60 ml (2 fl oz) in any one bottle (*see* pp.31–3).

Crying

Your baby may make her first cry as soon as her chest is delivered, or she may wait until she's been born and starts to breathe normally. These first cries are often no more than a whimper, with full-bodied crying following on later. It's perfectly normal for your baby to go bright red when she cries and to draw her knees up. Crying is your baby's way of communicating with you and you will soon notice that her cries when she is hungry are different to those she makes when she's tired or needs changing. It won't take you long to recognise why she is crying and how best to soothe her.

Sleeping

As your baby has no concept of night and day, there is no point in expecting her to sleep through the night and stay awake during the day. Some newborn babies sleep for 20 hours out of every 24, others sleep a lot less, but these periods of sleep and wakefulness can take place at any time. Your new baby may be a restless sleeper, throwing her arms and legs around even when she's deeply asleep, or she may sleep for hours with hardly any movement. Either way, normal household noises won't disturb her so you don't have to whisper and tiptoe around her. Although your baby may appear to be especially drowsy during the first few days, this will gradually give way to longer periods of alertness and physical activity.

A Moses basket or crib can provide your baby with a snug and comfortable bed until she is three to five months old.

Nappy contents

Your baby has a very small bladder, so you can expect her to pass urine up to 20 times a day at first. Don't be alarmed if her first nappies are stained dark pink, or even red. This occurs because after the birth her urine contains substances called urates. Your baby may also pass stools after each feed. These first stools will be a blackish-green colour as the meconium from the amniotic fluid she was drinking while in the uterus works its way out of her system. Once feeding begins, her stools will change to yellowish-orange if she is being breastfed, or pale brown if you're bottle feeding her.

Your baby's actions

Reflexes Your baby is born with a number of reflexes such as 'stepping', when she makes walking movements if you hold her upright with her feet on a flat surface, and grasping, where she demonstrates a surprisingly strong grip. A loud noise or the sensation of falling causes the startle, or Moro, reflex. This makes her extend her legs, arms and fingers while arching her back with her head thrown back, and then draw her arms, fists clenched, into her chest. Many of these initial reflexes gradually diminish over time as voluntary movements take their place.

The rooting reflex All babies are born with the rooting reflex, when their mouths automatically search for the nipple, as well as the ability to suck, swallow and gag. Gagging is especially important in a newborn baby as it prevents her from choking on too much liquid and allows her to get rid of any mucus that's blocking her airways.

Hiccups and snuffles Your baby is likely to hiccup and snuffle a lot at first, too. Hiccups occur because her breathing rhythm is still rather jerky, but as they won't hurt or even seem to bother her, they are not something you need to worry about, no matter how violent they look. Your baby's nasal passages are still very small and she snuffles as she learns to breathe through her nose. Although this can sound a bit alarming at first, it will soon stop as her nasal passages grow bigger. Bright lights stimulate the nerves in your baby's nose as well as her eyes, which is why she often sneezes when she first opens her eyes. Sneezing isn't a bad thing, though, as it helps to clear the nasal passages and prevents dust from getting into her lungs.

Sight and sound

Seeing Newborn babies prefer to look at a human face more than anything else, and it's thought they can recognise their mother's face just four hours after the birth. Although her vision is blurry, your baby can focus on items held around 20–30 cm (8–12 in) away, which is about the same distance as your face when you are holding and feeding her.

Hearing Your baby's hearing has been well developed for some time before birth, so she can distinguish between different types of sound and will start trying to determine where they come from by turning her head.

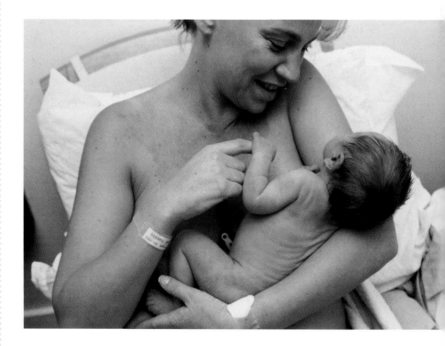

Your newborn baby can focus on your face almost immediately.

Medical care

Special care

If your baby has difficulties such as breathing problems after the birth or was born prematurely, she may need to go into a special care or neonatal unit. Most maternity departments have a special care nursery and some of these offer different levels of care.

How can you help?

Baby's first needs

❋ If your baby is in an incubator, stroke or hold her through the portholes. She will enjoy feeling your tender touch and it will help you too.

❋ Express breast milk so that she gets its benefits even if she can't suckle herself.

❋ Talk to your baby. She already knows your voice and will be comforted by it.

❋ You may be able to give 'kangaroo care'. This is where your baby is held against your chest so that she has skin-to-skin contact with you. Dads can do this, too.

Neonatal intensive care unit (NICU) This is for babies with the most severe problems and is where your baby will go if she was born before 34 weeks or needs a ventilator to help her with her breathing.

Special care baby unit (SCBU) Babies requiring a lower level of special care may go to this type of unit, so if your baby needs treatment such as for jaundice, or antibiotic treatment for an infection, she'll be looked after here.

Low dependency unit (LDU) Very often a baby will spend a short time being monitored in this type of unit after having been in NICU or SCBU.

If it's necessary for your baby to go into a special care unit for a period, you will meet the consultant paediatrician and midwife or nurse who will be responsible for your baby's treatment and who will be able to keep you informed about her progress. Although having your baby in any type of special care baby unit can't help but be distressing, do try to remember that these days the vast majority of babies who need special care go on to make a full recovery.

Seeing so much medical equipment surrounding your baby can be very distressing, but remember it ensures she gets the best treatment possible.

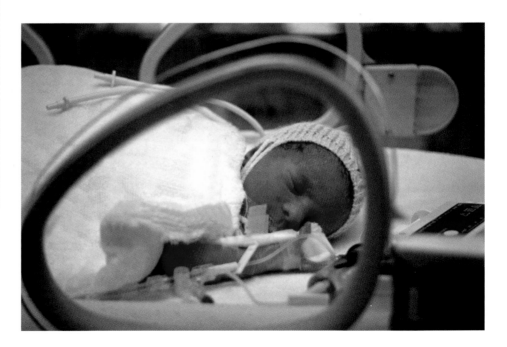

Spots, blemishes and birthmarks

Milia About 50 per cent of babies are born with milia, also known as milk rash. Caused by enlarged oil glands in the skin, these are white spots which look like tiny pimples on the baby's face, especially the nose. They disappear with time and are best left alone.

Stork marks These are collections of dilated blood vessels which appear as a red mark at the back of the baby's neck. Although they may never disappear completely, they are usually hidden by hair once it grows.

Salmon patches Similar in appearance to stork marks, these are usually found on the eyelids or on the forehead and will fade with time.

Strawberry marks These raised red marks are collections of blood capillaries. They often grow bigger before fading and then finally disappear at around five years of age. Unless they are in an awkward place they need no treatment and leave no lasting mark.

Mongolian blue spots These are caused by clusters of pigmentation cells and most commonly appear on the lower backs of dark-skinned babies as bruise-like bluish-grey patches. They usually disappear by school age.

Port wine stains Fortunately, these red or purple marks which appear on the face, head or neck are rare. They don't fade, but can usually be treated with laser therapy or plastic surgery.

Neonatal jaundice

Jaundice in newborn babies is very common – in fact it occurs in around 60 per cent of full-term babies and 80 per cent of premature babies. Jaundice (the yellowing of the skin and whites of the eyes) is not a disease but an indication of an underlying problem. In a newborn this is usually caused by high levels of a substance known as bilirubin in the blood. The liver, which is responsible for removing bilirubin from the blood, is often underdeveloped or immature in a newborn, especially if the baby is premature, so that the bilirubin isn't processed quickly enough and jaundice occurs. In rare cases jaundice is the sign of something more serious and further tests are required to establish the cause.

In most cases, the jaundice will disappear within a few days, usually without the need for any treatment. If treatment is needed, your baby may be placed under a harmless UV light which speeds up the metabolism of the excess bilirubin, a method known as phototherapy. Focused halogen lights and fibre-optic wrap-around blankets may also be used.

Breastfed babies can have prolonged jaundice which can last for three weeks or more. This rarely needs treatment and is not a reason for giving up breastfeeding.

A fibre-optic wrap-around blanket provides effective treatment for jaundice.

First check ups

A full examination will be carried out on your baby between 4 and 48 hours after the birth by a paediatrician, a midwife with special training in neonatal care or, if you have the baby at home, by a general practitioner (GP).

You will be asked about your family history and whether there were any problems during pregnancy which could affect your baby. Remember to include details of any abnormalities found during your antenatal scans as well as any family history such as dislocating hips in childhood or deafness. Your baby will then be examined (see panel, right).

The majority of babies pass this first examination with flying colours, but if there are any problems further tests or investigations may be required. If so, make sure you know what they are.

Apgar test

The first check your baby has is the Apgar test, which is given one minute after birth and again five minutes later. The midwife can usually do this test just by looking at your baby, so you may not be aware of it being carried out. The test is used to check a newborn's general condition to see if any treatment is needed. Your baby will score up to two points each for the following:

* activity and muscle tone
* pulse
* grimace reflex
* appearance and colour
* respiration.

If your baby scores between seven and ten she's in excellent condition, while a score of between four and six is fair but some resuscitative measures may be needed. If the score is below this, immediate treatment will be given. If your baby does require some help it's most likely to be a matter of clearing the airways, or giving her some oxygen to help her breathe.

Baby's first full check

Your baby will have the following examinations:

* her head circumference will be measured and the fontanelles will be checked
* a newborn hearing test will be given
* her eyes will be checked for cataracts and to make sure she has a 'red reflex'
* her mouth will be felt to make sure the roof of the mouth is complete
* her tongue will be checked for tongue-tie, a condition where the tongue remains more anchored to the bottom of the mouth than it should be
* a stethoscope will be used to listen to her heart in order to exclude heart murmurs
* her lungs will also be checked with a stethoscope to make sure that both are working properly
* her genitals will be checked and, in boys, the scrotum will be felt to make sure the testes have descended properly
* her skin will be examined for any birthmarks
* fingers and toes will be counted and checked for webbing. Her feet and ankles will be observed in a resting position for signs of talipes, or club foot
* her spine will be assessed for straightness
* her hips will be manipulated to check for any instability or 'clicky' hips
* her reflexes will be tested.

Help at home

Having some help in the early weeks after the birth is important as you'll be amazed at how tired you feel and how demanding your baby can be. If your partner can get time off work and is happy to share the chores and help you with the baby then he's the obvious choice. If this isn't possible, or if you'd feel happier having another female around, ask your mum, sister or a close girlfriend to lend a hand. Whether you have someone to stay for the first week or so, or just come in for a few hours each day, do be clear with them about the kind of help you want. If it's the chores you can't manage, make sure they understand that you want to spend your time concentrating on the baby. However, if you're finding new motherhood difficult to adjust to, you may be glad to hand over the baby for an hour or two.

Alternatively, you may prefer to employ someone for these early days after the birth. There are a number of choices available, from a full-time maternity nurse through to an au pair or mother's help. A maternity nurse is the most expensive, but she will live in and can be on duty 24 hours a day, 6 days a week. She often sleeps in the same room as the baby, bringing her in to you at night for a feed, or if you are bottle feeding, doing the night feeds herself so that you get plenty of rest. A maternity nurse is often a very experienced nanny with a special interest in newborn babies, although some may be registered nurses, ex-midwives or health visitors. She will provide total care for the mother and baby but won't involve herself in household chores or looking after other children.

A postnatal doula is becoming a popular choice. She will come into your home for a few hours a day to help you with your baby and to do light housework and shopping; she may even look after other children. Experienced in caring for postnatal mothers and their babies, she will be able to advise you about feeding, starting a routine and how best to look after yourself. A postnatal doula is usually paid by the hour.

Night-time assistance

If it's only the night feeds and lack of sleep that are getting you down, a night nanny could be the answer. This is a nanny who comes to your home in the evening and stays through until around seven or eight o'clock in the morning. During this time she will either bring the baby to you to breastfeed or provide bottle feeds herself, and she will change and settle the baby after each feed. A night nanny is usually paid by the night.

An au pair or a mother's help will be someone who is usually untrained in childcare, apart from perhaps having had the care of younger siblings, so you can't expect expert advice to help you with your newborn. However, she can help with the household chores and will be able to keep an eye on other children. An au pair or a mother's help should probably be employed in good time before the birth to give her a chance to get accustomed to your home before the baby is born. Her hours and wages are usually negotiated and agreed before she starts work.

Night-time feeds give dads the perfect opportunity to bond with their newborns, so ask your partner to take responsibility for some of them, especially if you are suffering badly with sleep deprivation.

Week 1

Your baby's progress

Your baby will probably spend most of his time feeding or sleeping. When he feeds you will be able to see some of the reflexes he was born with come into play as he roots for the nipple or teat, then sucks and swallows the milk you offer him. Use this time to bond with your baby by talking and singing to him and caressing him. You'll be surprised at how much he responds, even at this early age.

When your baby isn't sleeping or feeding his main activity will be sucking and chewing his hands. The large number of touch receptors in his hands and lips makes this an enjoyable and comforting pastime for him. If he scratches his face, you may want to put baby mitts on his hands at night. His movements may be rather jerky and uncoordinated, but this will change over the next few weeks as his muscle tone matures.

Your baby was able to hear when he was in the womb, so he can distinguish sounds and voices. The nerves connecting vision and hearing are already developed, so he will turn towards the source of a noise. However, his sight still has some way to go before it is fully developed, so right now he sees better close up. Hold a brightly coloured rattle 20–25 cm (8–10 in) from his face and shake it on one side of his head and then on the other; watch him seek it out with his eyes as he turns his head towards the sound.

Your baby will be fascinated by high-contrast objects like this black and white bear. Hold the toy close so that she can focus on it easily.

Parents' survival guide

Mums

You'll be coming to terms with your post-pregnancy body and, although you'll probably be looking a lot slimmer now, you may be disappointed that you can't get back into your favourite jeans just yet. Don't be disheartened – it usually takes a while for your figure to return to something like its pre-pregnancy shape.

Your perineum is likely to be the most painful area of your body after birth, especially if you've had stitches. If sitting is uncomfortable take paracetamol and try using a soothing gel pack. You'll need to wear maternity pads because of the period-like discharge you'll be having (tampons are not recommended because of the risk of infection). Called lochia, this discharge will be heavy at first but it will gradually diminish over the next few weeks. If it becomes smelly or appears muckier than usual, contact your midwife or doctor as you may have an infection.

You may experience cramp-like after-pains as your uterus shrinks back to normal size. These are often worse when you're breastfeeding. A day or two after the birth you will probably find yourself feeling unusually weepy. Caused by hormonal changes, this often occurs at the same time as your milk 'comes in' (see p.23).

Dads

You're likely to find your partner on an emotional rollercoaster this week as her hormone levels drop dramatically after the birth, so be prepared for both tears and laughter. Be reassuring and supportive if she is struggling with breastfeeding and encourage her to ask the midwife or health visitor for help if it's needed. Lack of sleep can come as a shock to both of you, but try not to let it get you down. It shouldn't be too long before your baby starts sleeping for longer periods at night.

You are likely to have a large number of visitors, all anxious to see your new baby. This can be tiring, especially for your partner, so keep any visits short and don't be afraid to ask people to come another day if your partner is showing signs of fatigue.

Milestones for week 1

Your baby...

* can distinguish between faces and patterns
* prefers high-pitched voices
* will want to feed frequently
* is likely to be producing at least eight to twelve wet nappies a day
* should start to regain some of the weight he lost after the birth.

You...

* are now producing milk in response to your baby's needs
* are likely to be experiencing 'after-pains' as the uterus begins to contract to its normal size, especially when you breastfeed
* will have a period-like discharge known as lochia
* may be feeling weepy and emotional because of the changes in your hormone levels
* should have a visit from your community midwife or health visitor this week.

Holding and handling your baby

Your baby may appear tiny and fragile at first, making you nervous about handling him in case you accidentally do something to hurt him. However, babies are a lot tougher than they look, and provided you treat him gently and make sure that his head and neck are well supported there is no reason why you should cause him any discomfort. In fact, your baby will actively enjoy being held close to you – though he may not like sudden movements, so keep any changes of position smooth and gentle. Even if you are feeling nervous, try to hold your baby confidently so that he feels secure.

A good position for soothing or carrying your baby when he's sleepy is to hold him on your shoulder with his body upright and his head resting against you. Support his upper back with one hand and his bottom with the other.

When you cradle your baby in your arms, rest his head just above the crook of one arm, with your lower arm supporting his body and your other hand under his bottom. Hold your baby so that his head is slightly higher than his bottom. If your baby is happiest when he's in your arms, you might want to consider using a sling some of the time so that he is held close to you even when you are getting on with other things.

Your baby will feel very secure when he is held close to you, and will enjoy your smell and the sound of your voice.

Handle with care

You should never shake your baby, either deliberately or unintentionally in the course of playing with him. His head is quite heavy and his neck and back muscles are not strong enough to hold it up unaided. If you shake him his head will snap backwards and forwards, which could tear blood vessels in his brain and cause brain damage – in severe cases, even death. Many accidents at home are associated with people having drunk alcohol, so be especially careful with your baby if you've had a drink.

Swaddling

This is an age-old method for soothing a baby if he is unsettled or distressed. Not all babies like it, but if yours does, it can be a very good way of calming him down. Do remember that if you put your swaddled baby down to sleep, you must keep a check on him to make sure that he doesn't become overheated.

1 Fold a cot sheet or cotton blanket into a triangular shape and place it on a flat surface. Lay your baby on the top of it with the back of his neck in the middle of the long edge.

2 Bring one side of the sheet diagonally across your baby's shoulder and tuck it under his body, leaving his arm on that side free. The sheet should be snug, but not pulled too tight.

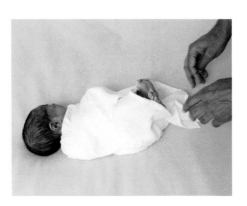

3 Then bring the remaining side across his uncovered shoulder and tuck that under the opposite side of his body. He will now feel held, which will make him feel secure.

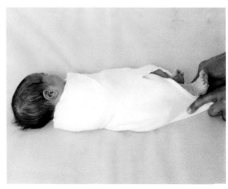

4 You can tuck the bottom end of the sheet up under your baby's feet, or leave it loose.

Some early concerns

It's quite natural to have concerns about some of the physical aspects of caring for your newborn. You may also be worried about whether you are doing the 'right' thing in letting him have the tests that he'll be offered to check that he is healthy. Your midwife or health visitor is there to help you and will be able to reassure you about any worries that you may have.

The umbilical cord

The area surrounding the stump of the umbilical cord doesn't need any special treatment apart from being kept clean and dry. It doesn't matter if it gets wet during bathtime as long as you pat it dry carefully afterwards. Many newborn nappies have a shaped cut-out section which allows the cord to remain uncovered so that the air can reach it, helping it to heal faster. Otherwise just make sure that the nappy is folded so that the cord is free. In the past, talcum powder was used routinely to help dry the area, but it sometimes seems to cause irritation so it's best avoided. The stump will drop off five to ten days after the birth, leaving a small wound that will take a few days to heal.

You should contact your doctor or health visitor immediately if there is any bleeding or discharge from the stump or around its base, or if the area becomes red or swollen, as this could be a sign of an infection. A bulging navel may indicate an umbilical hernia (more common in African and Afro-Caribbean babies). Nearly all umbilical hernias correct themselves by the time the child is two to three years old, but occasionally surgery is required after this age to strengthen the area around the navel and hold in the bulge. Generally, surgery is only recommended if the hernia hasn't gone away by the time the child is three or if it has progressively worsened over this period.

Guthrie test

This is a 'heel-prick' blood test which is carried out on a baby 5 to 14 days after birth. It screens your baby's blood for signs of a rare, but treatable, metabolic disease called phenylketonuria (an inability to digest protein) and hypothyroidism (thyroid deficiency). In some parts of the country the blood sample is also used to check for cystic fibrosis (a condition that affects the lungs and digestive system) and for sickle cell anaemia and milder sickle cell disorders.

Feeding needs to be well-established before the Guthrie test is carried out, so if you are having any feeding difficulties the test may be delayed for a day or two. The test results usually take around three weeks to arrive.

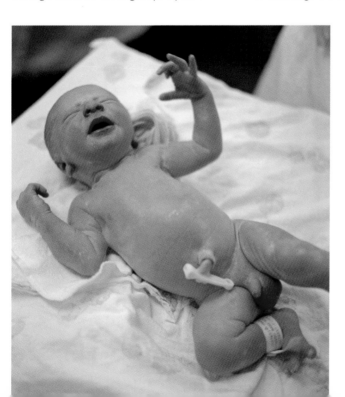

The cord stump can look strange, but it will drop off a few days after the birth, revealing your baby's navel.

Vitamin K level

One in 10,000 babies is born with low levels of vitamin K (which is vital for blood clotting). Because of this doctors recommend that all babies should be given vitamin K, but the final decision as to whether your baby has it or not is yours. The vitamin can be given as an injection shortly after delivery or orally during the first week, followed by a second dose at seven days and a further dose at 29 days if you are breastfeeding. If you have any concerns about your baby having vitamin K, talk to your midwife or doctor.

Living in the real world is a massive change for a baby that has just spent nine months inside you. This helps to explain why most babies lose weight in their first week.

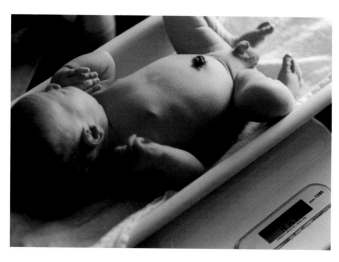

Early weight loss

It is perfectly normal for your baby to lose weight during the first few days after birth. He will then start to put it back on so that any weight loss will be regained over the next two weeks. From then on your baby will probably gain weight regularly, though this is likely to be at varying rates.

Cranial osteopathy

During birth a baby's head is compressed and moulded to fit through the birth canal. After delivery the head starts to 'un-mould', but in some cases this doesn't always happen quickly, especially if the delivery was assisted. This can lead to the nerves in the skull being irritated, so that the baby becomes fractious as a result.

Cranial osteopathy, a gentle 'touch' therapy, is often used to decompress the joins in the skull so that the baby gets relief and becomes more comfortable and settled. Cranial osteopathy can also be used successfully to help with colic, feeding difficulties, sickness and wind problems, and sleep disturbances. If your baby appears unsettled and discontented ask your health visitor about cranial osteopathy, or talk to a qualified practitioner in your area. For further information, and to find a cranial osteopath registered with the General Osteopathic Council, contact the Sutherland Society at www.cranial.org.uk.

Keeping a record

Your baby's weight, height and head circumference will be entered in your baby's Personal Child Health Record (known in some places as the 'Red Book'). This is a record book which is held by you and filled in by any health professionals who see your baby at regular check-ups during his first few years. His height and weight will be plotted on centile charts which work on averages. (So, for example, being on the 50th centile for height means your baby is average for his age. Similarly, being on the 90th centile for height indicates that your baby is tall for his age.) Do remember that most babies, like adults, are not average.

Breastfeeding basics

You may imagine that breastfeeding will just happen naturally without any special effort on your part, but this isn't always the case. Some women do sail through breastfeeding without any problems, but many more have to learn this new skill and, like all skills, it comes more easily to some than to others. Although your baby is born with a sucking reflex and your breasts will naturally produce milk after the birth, you have to learn how to position your baby so that he can 'latch on' properly. This means that his mouth has formed a tight seal over your nipple and most of your areola (the brown area surrounding the nipple). If your baby isn't latched on correctly he will chew or suck on your nipple, making it sore, and he won't be getting enough milk.

When your baby feeds, a hormone called oxytocin is released in you. This stimulates the 'let-down' reflex which squeezes the milk out of the glands and into the milk ducts. Once this is working well, usually by the second week, your breasts will work more efficiently so that your baby will find feeding easy. If the let-down reflex isn't working as well as it should your breasts may not be emptied at the end of a feed and your baby may not be getting enough milk.

If you experience difficulties at first, don't be tempted to give up. Even if your baby is screaming the place down and you are in tears of frustration, try to remember that the majority of breastfeeding problems can be easily overcome with the right help and

support, so ask your midwife, health visitor or a breastfeeding counsellor for advice. With a bit of perseverance you'll be able to do it and, once you've mastered the skill, you'll find it convenient and hassle-free, as well as a wonderfully satisfying experience.

Why breastfeed?

Breastfeeding is best for your baby because:

❃ your baby will ingest antibodies that protect from infections such as gastroenteritis, respiratory illness and urinary tract and ear infections

❃ it reduces the risk of childhood diabetes

❃ it helps to prevent allergic conditions such as eczema

❃ your child is less likely to be obese in later life

❃ it lowers the risk of heart disease in adulthood.

The benefits of breastfeeding for you are:

❃ it will help your body recover its pre-pregnancy shape more quickly after the birth

❃ it reduces the risk of pre-menopausal breast cancer

❃ it gives protection from osteoporosis and ovarian cancer.

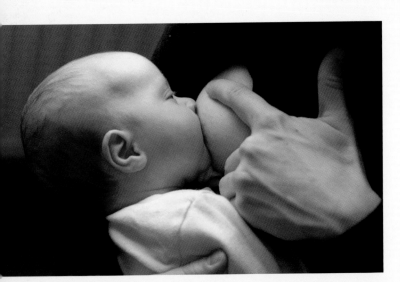

Breastfeeding promotes bonding between mother and baby and provides many valuable health benefits for both, too.

Breast milk

The milk from your breasts contains all the nutrients your baby needs, in the right quantities, for the first six months of his life, so ideally your baby should be breastfed until he is at least six months old, and for longer if this is possible in practical terms. Breast milk is produced on a supply and demand basis – the more your baby needs the more your breasts provide. During this first week you should feed your baby whenever he seems hungry, which could be as frequently as 6 to 12 times in every 24 hours.

The first 'milk' your breasts produce after the birth is called colostrum. This is a high-protein liquid rich in the antibodies that will give your baby protection from infection and help to build a strong immune system. It is followed a few days later by transitional milk, which is a mixture of colostrum and mature breast milk. Your breasts are likely to feel full and uncomfortable during this change, a stage which is often described as 'the milk coming in'. Feeding your baby frequently will help to ease the pressure and any discomfort should wear off after a couple of days.

Mature breast milk is made up of fore milk and hind milk. The fore milk, which your baby gets at the start of a feed, is thin and watery and designed to quench his thirst. This is then followed by the nutritionally rich hind milk, which satisfies his hunger. It's important that you always let your baby suckle for as long as he wants from the first breast so that he gets plenty of the satisfying hind milk before moving him on to the second breast. If he sucks for less than ten minutes he's likely to be hungry again very soon. You will know when the breast is empty as it will look smaller and feel lighter when the milk has gone.

If you have to remove your baby from the breast, don't try pulling him off as this will make your nipple sore. Instead, insert your clean little finger into his mouth to break the suction. Alternate the breast you offer first so that both get a similar amount of stimulation over a 24-hour period.

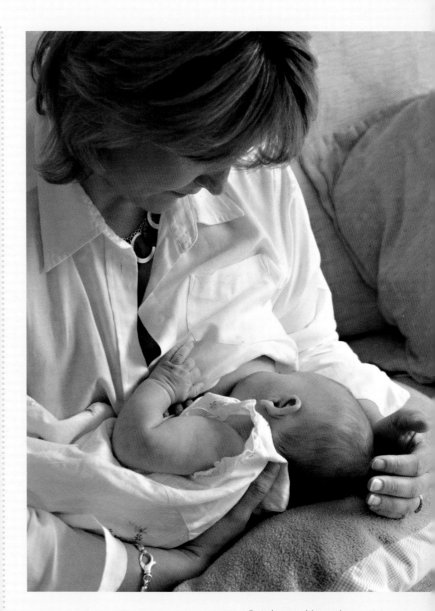

Experiment with a variety of positions when you breastfeed, to find the ones that work best for both you and your baby.

Getting your baby latched on

Feeds can take any time from ten minutes to an hour, so it's really important to be comfortable. Choose a chair that supports your back or lie down on the bed or sofa.

Latched on?

Your baby isn't properly latched on if:

* his cheeks are sucked in while he feeds
* he makes clicking noises or smacks his lips during a feed
* your breast or nipple hurts.

For advice on overcoming breastfeeding problems, *see* p.50.

1 You may find it helpful to place your baby on a pillow so that you can draw him onto the breast without straining. Once you are settled, hold your baby in a straight line with your breast so that he doesn't need to turn his head to feed. His nose should be in line with your nipple and he should be able to see you with the eye nearest to your face.

2 Now encourage him to open his mouth by stroking his mouth with your nipple. Once his mouth is wide open, draw him towards you so that he takes the breast deeply into his mouth. His bottom lip should make first contact with the breast, well away from the base of the nipple. To feed successfully he needs to have all the nipple and most of the areola in his mouth so that he can massage the milk from the breast. It's important to remember that he should be breastfeeding, not just nipple sucking.

3 If your baby is latched on successfully his mouth will be wide open with his lower lip turned down and he should have more of the breast below the nipple than above it in his mouth. His cheek should just be touching your breast while his chin presses into it, keeping his nose clear. You should be able to see his jaw working as he sucks and you may notice his sucking pattern change from small quick gulps to longer, deeper swallows.

Feeding after a Caesarian

There is no reason why you can't breastfeed after a Caesarean – in fact, if you had an epidural it's a good idea to start before the effects of the anaesthetic have worn off.

Finding a comfortable nursing position is the key to success, so take your time to find out what suits you. Many mothers find the 'football hold' comfortable. This is where a cushion or pillow is used to protect the caesarian scar and support the weight of the baby.

1 Sit in an upright position with your baby supported on a pillow so that he is level with your nipple, with his body lying along the length of your forearm and his face towards your breast. Gently holding his head with your hand, draw him onto the breast using your other hand to position your nipple in his mouth.

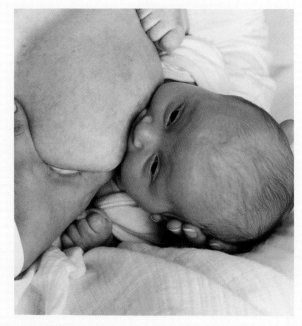

2 Once your baby is latched on and sucking well you may want to adjust the pillow he's lying on so that it also supports the hand that is holding his head.

Week 2

Your baby's progress

Long periods of drowsiness will gradually start giving way to longer periods of alertness and physical activity. Your baby will probably spend this 'awake' time stretching out and then drawing in her arms and legs, sucking her hands or staring intently at a colourful moving object such as a mobile hung over the cot or a brightly coloured toy being shaken within her field of vision.

Some of the reflexes she has been born with, such as stepping and swimming, will become the foundation for the motor skills your baby will need when she's older. The stepping movements you can see now when you hold her upright with her feet on a hard surface will become walking, while the swimming reflex will eventually lead to crawling.

Your baby has begun to recognise your face and will respond to you with pleasure when you are talking to her. You can build on this growing sense of attachment by responding to her needs, for example by feeding her when she cries for food, so that she doesn't become distressed by feelings of hunger. This early attachment or 'bonding' will help to develop your

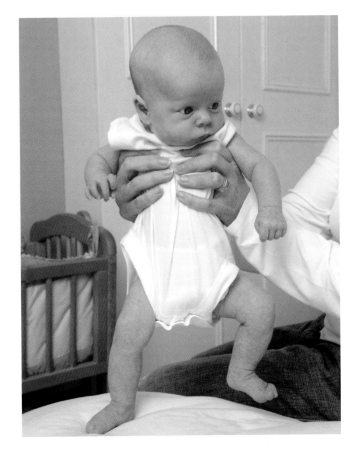

You can encourage your baby to develop her stepping reflex by holding her upright on a flat surface.

baby's confidence and security which will, in turn, help her to thrive and learn.

It's not too early to start having a two-way conversation with your baby. Try imitating the cooing noises she makes and copy her facial expressions while holding eye contact with her. If you watch closely you will be able to see and hear her responses. This dialogue will later become the basis for your baby's communication skills.

Parents' survival guide

Mums

Your community midwife will probably visit you at home soon after the birth. She's there to help you through these first days, so she'll want to know how you are feeling, how your baby is feeding and what problems – if any – you are having. She'll also want to keep a check on you to make sure that your body is recovering well after the birth, so expect her to ask a lot of personal questions such as how your bowels are working and whether you are urinating frequently.

At some time between 10 and 28 days a health visitor will take over your care and that of your baby. Her role is to help families, especially those with babies and young children, to keep healthy. She will come and see you at home before arranging for you to take your baby to the baby clinic for future check-ups. Some health visitors also run special clinics for sleep and behavioural problems.

Your community midwife and health visitor are part of the network of health professionals who are there to support you. How many routine visits you receive often depends on how well you are coping. If there are complications or you're finding it hard to manage, you're likely to see them more frequently.

Dads

You may be on paternity leave this week. It is your legal right (subject to conditions) to take one or two consecutive weeks off work within eight weeks of the birth. In the majority of cases this is paid leave, usually at the same rate as statutory maternity pay (SMP).

As government regulations on paternity leave, along with other family entitlements, are updated quite frequently you'll need to keep a check on what you're entitled to. Your employer, trade union, local Jobcentre, Social Security office or Citizen's Advice Bureau (CAB) will be able to give you all the up-to-date information. You can also check out the DTI website, www.dti.gov.uk.

Milestones for week 2

Your baby...

* will be starting to uncurl from her newborn position
* may exhibit signs of recognising your face
* can make a walking movement when she is held upright on a hard surface
* will stay awake and be alert for longer periods
* will start trying to communicate with you.

You...

* may be getting used to breastfeeding as your milk supply settles down
* may feel the 'let down' reflex response to your baby's cries
* will be learning to adjust to the demands of motherhood
* will probably be feeling very tired
* will need to practise your pelvic floor exercises every day to strengthen these muscles.

Winding

Some babies are very windy, while others hardly seem to be troubled by wind at all. Wind is the air that your baby swallows when feeding, crying or yawning, and it has to escape from one end or the other. Trapped wind can make your baby very uncomfortable – you'll see her draw up her knees, go red in the face and become distressed. If she's swallowing a lot of wind during a feed she's also likely to feel fuller than she really is, so that once the wind has been passed she'll be hungry again. Burping your baby halfway through a feed and again at the end by gently stroking or patting her back will help her bring up wind.

Reflux

Sometimes acid from a baby's stomach flows back up the throat along with some milk during or after a feed, causing reflux. Reflux may produce colicky-type symptoms, so it is often mistakenly diagnosed as colic. However, many babies with reflux seem to bring up feeds effortlessly and without discomfort and are happy to start feeding again straight away. If your baby has reflux your doctor may prescribe a specially formulated child's antacid to soothe the discomfort and you may be advised to hold your baby upright as much as possible so that there is less chance of the acid making its way up into the throat. You may also find that it helps to raise the head of the cot slightly so that your baby isn't lying completely flat when asleep. Try putting books under the feet. Babies usually grow out of reflux by the end of the first year. (For information on colic see p.42.)

To relieve wind, hold your baby upright and support her head and chest with one hand while you gently rub or pat her back with the other.

Possetting

It's quite normal for a baby to bring back some milk during or after a feed. Provided your baby is thriving and putting on weight, this 'possetting' or 'spitting up' is usually nothing to worry about. Even if your baby brings back what seems like a lot of milk, apart from becoming hungry again more quickly, this usually doesn't do her any harm – though it can give you a frequently wet shoulder.

However, you should talk to your doctor or health visitor if your baby seems to be in pain or doesn't seem to be thriving, or if she gags a lot during a feed or produces sick that looks more like vomit than curdled milk.

Possetting points

❋ Protect your baby's clothes with a bib and have a muslin cloth handy for mopping up.

❋ If you're formula feeding, check the hole in the teat isn't too big – it should produce two to three drops a second when the bottle is held upside down.

❋ Changing to an anti-colic teat may reduce the amount of air she takes in.

❋ If you're breastfeeding, make sure your baby is latched on properly.

❋ Wind your baby halfway through a feed as well as afterwards.

❋ Don't jog her about immediately after she's finished feeding.

Muslin cloths help to protect your clothes from the milk your baby spits up. You'll need to have a plentiful supply of them.

Sleeping safely

Cot death (Sudden Infant Death Syndrome) – when a baby dies suddenly for no apparent reason – is a huge worry to new parents, although, thankfully, it happens very rarely. You can reduce the risk of cot death and help your baby sleep safely by following these tips:

❋ always place your baby to sleep on her back, in the 'feet-to-foot' position (see picture below) so that she can't wriggle down under the covers and become overheated

❋ put your baby down to sleep in her own crib or cot but keep her with you in your bedroom for the first six months

❋ keep the room where she sleeps at a constant temperature – the ideal is 16–18 °C (60–64 °F)

❋ never take your baby into bed with you if you've been drinking alcohol or taking any form of drugs, or if you are over-tired – you could fall asleep and suffocate your baby

❋ don't put her cot in direct sunlight or next to a radiator as she may become overheated

❋ make sure that the mattress she sleeps on is firm and don't use pillows, a duvet or a cot bumper until she's at least one year old

❋ don't allow anyone to smoke in the house, especially not in the room with your baby

❋ never use an electric blanket or hot water bottle in your baby's crib or cot

❋ if your baby seems unwell, is hotter than usual and has lost interest in her feeds, seek urgent medical advice.

Put your baby down to sleep on her back, with her feet at the bottom of the crib or cot and the covers tucked in no higher than her shoulders.

Flattened head syndrome

Also known as deformational plagiocephaly or plagio, flattened head syndrome occurs when pressure causes the soft bones of the head to become flattened. It has become more common since the recommendation that babies should sleep on their backs. While it can look unsightly, there is no evidence that it is in any way dangerous.

Although it can't be prevented completely, and in most cases it rights itself as the child gets older, there are ways of improving your baby's head shape:

❋ alter the position of toys and mobiles to encourage your baby to move her head away from the flattened side

❋ move a night-light to alternate sides of the cot each night as babies always look towards the light

❋ reposition your baby's head away from the flattened side once she's asleep

❋ encourage your baby to spend time each day playing on her stomach. Tummy play will also help to strengthen the neck muscles

❋ try to reduce the amount of time spent with her head on a firm surface such as a car seat or buggy

❋ use front rather than back carriers.

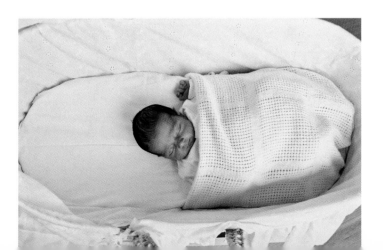

Bottle feeding

Although breast milk is the best and most natural food, you may choose to give your baby infant formula. The important thing is to be happy with your decision. Just because you're giving your baby a bottle rather than your breast doesn't mean that the experience should be any the less enjoyable for either of you, so make the most of each feed by settling comfortably and giving your baby all your attention.

At first you'll need to feed your baby on demand, which could be every hour or two during the early days. Start by offering 60 ml (2 fl oz) and then be guided by your baby – she won't finish a bottle if she doesn't want it and she'll make it obvious if she's still hungry. As the amount she takes at each feed increases over the course of the next few weeks, the time between feeds will lengthen until there is a three to four hour gap between each one.

The right formula

Formula milk is usually based upon cow's milk and will provide your baby with all the vitamins and minerals she needs for the first six months. Although there are a number of brands to choose from, there are two main types of formula milk – first-stage milks which are mainly whey-based, and casein-based milks for older or hungrier babies

(these are not recommended for young babies). Your midwife or health visitor will be the best person to advise you on which formula is the most suitable for your baby.

Formula usually comes as a powder, although some brands are available ready-made in small cartons – ideal for travelling and emergencies but an expensive option for everyday use. If there is a family history of lactose intolerance or allergies connected to cow's milk, it may be suggested that you use a specially designed milk, but check with your GP first. Goat's milk formula has not been approved by the Department of Health in the UK so should never be given to your baby.

Feeding equipment

As well as infant formula you will need at least:
* six bottles
* six teats
* a bottle brush
* sterilising equipment.

Hygiene

It's really important that all your baby's bottles and teats are sterilised before use because of the risk of infection – particularly gastroenteritis, which can be very dangerous for babies. Bottles should be washed using a bottle brush in warm soapy water and then rinsed well. Teats need to be turned inside out and then thoroughly washed with water run through the hole to make sure there are no traces of milk left in them. Once the teats and bottles are clean they need to be sterilised. There are several ways of doing this:

* use an electric steam steriliser
* use a microwave steriliser
* use sterilising solution
* boil the equipment in a large pan for a minimum of ten minutes.

An electric steam steriliser.

Making up a feed

Preparing a bottle may seem time-consuming at first but it will soon become second nature. It is vital not to skimp on any part of the procedure.

1   Wash and dry your hands. Now fill the kettle with fresh water and bring it to the boil while you check that the bottle, cap, teat and disc are sterilised and ready for use. Allow the water to cool to about 70 °C (158 °F) before pouring the required amount into the bottle.

2   Add the correct amount of formula (details are on the pack), using the scoop provided. To ensure that you don't over- or under-fill the scoop, level it off with the back of a sterilised knife. It's vital to follow the instructions on the pack as the wrong ratio of formula to water could harm your baby.

3   Put the teat or disc in the neck of the bottle and screw the cap on tightly before shaking until all the powder has dispersed. Hold the bottle under the cold tap to cool it to the right temperature for your baby. The bottle is now ready.

Bottle-feeding know-how

❋ Once boiled, the water should be left to cool for no more than 30 minutes.

❋ If you want to rinse the bottle and teat before making up formula, always use boiled water.

❋ Make up one bottle at a time and cool it quickly by running it under a cold tap. If you are not using it immediately, store it in the refrigerator below 5 °C (41 °F). Made-up formula shouldn't be out of the refrigerator for any longer than one hour.

❋ If you're going away from home, take a sterilised thermos flask of freshly boiled water and the correct amount of formula in a separate container. Mix together when your baby needs feeding.

❋ Never reheat or re-use made-up formula. If your baby has only had a small amount, throw away what's left.

❋ Never use formula which is past its 'best before' date.

❋ Don't leave your baby alone with a bottle – she could easily choke.

❋ Never add anything to the bottle such as baby rice. If your baby seems hungry at the end of a feed talk to your health visitor, who may recommend a different formula.

❋ Some babies prefer their milk at room temperature, while others like theirs warm. If you need to heat the bottle, place it in a bowl of hot water or use an electric bottle warmer. Don't heat a bottle in a microwave oven as it can cause 'hot spots' which could burn your baby's mouth.

❋ Don't dilute the feed with more water if you think your baby is thirsty. If your baby needs to drink more, offer cooled boiled water on its own between normal feeds.

❋ You can find further information on bottle-feeding on the NHS Direct website, www.nhsdirect.nhs.uk.

Feeding your baby

Make yourself comfortable and hold your baby close to your body with her head resting in the crook of your arm so that you can look into her eyes and talk to her while she feeds. Shake the bottle to make sure the temperature is even and place a few drops on the inside of your wrist to check the temperature – it should feel warm, but not hot, on your skin. Hold the bottle so that the teat is filled with milk and not air. If the teat collapses, gently remove it from your baby's mouth so that the air can get back into the bottle.

The more time a dad can spend with his baby, the more effectively the two of them will bond. Bottle feeding is one way for a father to spend quality time with his newborn and to take part in caring for her.

Weight gain

Weight gain for both boys and girls is quickest during the first six to nine months and then slows down. Most babies double their birth weight by six months and treble it by one year.

At first breastfed babies may put on more weight than babies who are formula-fed, then at around four months this begins to change so that between six months and one year formula-fed babies are usually ahead in the weight-gaining stakes.

You may find your baby is weighed regularly at the baby clinic, or it may be done only when you request it. Each weigh-in will be recorded on centile charts in your baby's Personal Child Health Record book. There are separate charts for boys and girls, as boys are, on average, heavier and taller, and their growth pattern is slightly different from that of girls. These charts are based on data for normal, healthy children (special charts are available for other groups) and are intended to be used only as a guide to help you track your child's progress.

It's quite normal for your baby to gain weight one week and then not gain any the next. Don't panic if this happens; it's the general weight gain over a period of weeks that matters. If you have any concern about your child's weight gain, talk to your health visitor or doctor.

Week 3

Your baby's progress

Your baby is gradually gaining control of his muscles, so you'll notice his arm and leg movements become less jerky. He will enjoy kicking and grabbing at things, even though he isn't yet sufficiently coordinated to grasp them. Watch his legs go when you put him down on his back and pick him up, or while he's in the bath. If you put him down on his front now he may be able to lift his head briefly, as his neck muscles are becoming stronger. He may even try turning it from side to side.

Your baby learns a lot through simply watching and listening to you. You can help him become familiar with the pattern of language by chatting to him whenever he's awake, using simple sentences and lots of repetition. Babies love to mimic and you can encourage him by pulling faces and then waiting to see if he tries to copy you. It may take time for him to catch on, but if you keep smiling at your baby, with a broad exaggerated grin, you should be rewarded with a smile in return over the next week or two.

Although initially crying was a reflex, your baby is now beginning to use crying as a form of communication. Listen to the

Try making faces at your three-week-old and see whether or not you get a response. Encourage her to mirror your face by using lots of positive sounds and gestures.

difference between his cries of hunger and the crying he does when he is tired or his nappy needs changing. Over time you'll be able to differentiate between them and, once you've learnt to interpret his different cries, you'll be able to understand what he's trying to tell you.

Parents' survival guide

Mums

If you had a Caesarean birth you'll be starting to feel a bit more comfortable now, although it will be six weeks before you are considered fit and it can take a further four or five months before you are fully recovered. It's important to take things easy when you get home from the hospital, so try to get as much help as possible over the next few weeks. It's especially important not to lift or carry anything heavy, and this includes older children, so you may need to enlist some help with childcare while you concentrate on getting better and looking after your baby.

Although you're probably anxious to lose the extra pounds you put on during pregnancy, when you've had a Caesarean any form of exercise programme should wait until six to eight weeks after delivery. Even then, you should start slowly and gradually build up the amount that you do.

It used to be the case that women weren't allowed to drive for six weeks after a Caesarean, but things are a bit more relaxed these days as power steering has made cars a lot easier and lighter to drive. If your doctor agrees, you may be able to drive after three to four weeks, but do check that this is acceptable to your insurance company. You'll find that once you start driving again the biggest strain is managing to get your baby's car seat in and out of the car. Do be careful when you do this and, if possible, find someone else to do it for you.

Dads

Your partner is likely to be feeling sore and tired for a few more weeks, so she'll need a lot of help and support, especially if you already have children. Perhaps you could organise a rota of people – family and friends – who could be around to help when you are at work. If you don't already do this, you may want to consider shopping online for your groceries. All the larger supermarkets offer this service and will deliver your shopping to your door at a time that's convenient.

Milestones for week 3

Your baby...

* may be beginning to develop more regular sleeping and eating patterns
* enjoys nursery rhymes and simple phrases with lots of repetition
* likes being held close to you and may enjoy being carried in a sling on your front
* may be able to lift his head up briefly and even turn it from side to side
* is trying to communicate with you with different cries.

You...

* could be experiencing emotional ups and downs. Talk to your health visitor if these 'baby blues' are becoming a problem
* are probably feeling exhausted as broken nights take their toll. Try to sleep when your baby does, regardless of the time of day
* should be eating a healthy, well-balanced diet
* need to go for a brisk walk in the fresh air at least once a day.

Topping and tailing

Young babies often object quite noisily to being undressed and immersed in water, so don't feel you have to bath your baby every day – unless she enjoys it, of course. Babies of this age don't really get dirty, so a 'top and tail' wash is all that's needed until you both feel more comfortable about bathing.

3 Your baby's ears and nose are self-cleaning, so never try cleaning inside them. Just gently remove any visible wax or mucus with a piece of damp cotton wool or a cotton bud. Once you have washed her face, clean in the folds of her neck, then use a fresh piece of cotton wool to dry the area.

1 The room should be warm and draught-free and you should have everything you need ready before you start. Place your baby on a changing mat or towel and remove the top half of her clothing, leaving her nappy in place.

4 Using fresh pads of cotton wool, wash in the creases underneath your baby's arms. Then, using another piece of cotton wool gently dry the area.

2 Always start by washing your baby's face with cooled boiled water, using several pieces of cotton wool. Then, taking fresh pieces of cotton wool, gently wipe each eye, starting from the inner corner and working outwards.

5 Now, wash between your baby's fingers to remove any trapped dirt or fluff and then dry her hands carefully with more fresh cotton wool.

6 Put your baby in a clean vest, and pull it down only as far as her waist so that the bottom of it is out of the way of the nappy. You're now ready to 'tail' her – wash her bottom half.

Equipment

When topping and tailing you will need:
* a bowl of cooled boiled water
* a changing mat or towel
* cotton wool
* cotton buds (optional)
* Barrier cream (optional)
* a clean nappy, a vest and baby clothes.

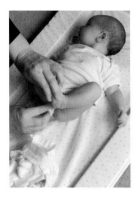

7 Gently clean her bottom with damp cotton wool, making sure that you clean in all the creases. Don't try to clean inside your baby girl's vulva as this could introduce infection. Always wipe from front to back so as not to spread bacteria from the anus to the vagina. When cleaning a boy, never pull the foreskin back – it's still stuck to his penis, so could be damaged. Always wipe his penis downwards, away from his body, and make sure you clean around his testicles as well. Dry the area and apply a small amount of barrier cream if necessary.

8 Once your baby is ready to have her clean nappy on, gently lift her legs so that you can place it under her bottom, then draw it up between her legs. Fasten the nappy, making sure that the waist and legs fit snugly, but not too tightly. Now pull your baby's vest down over the nappy and secure the poppers between her legs. Your baby is now clean and comfortable and ready to be dressed again.

Circumcision

Boys are born with foreskin – skin that covers the end of their penis. Your religious beliefs may dictate that the foreskin be removed soon after birth. Known as circumcision, this operation is minor and very straightforward, but it does usually cause some swelling or bleeding and you will need to watch for signs of infection. Until the area is completely healed you should try to keep the penis as dry as possible.

Some parents want to have their son circumcised because they believe it is more hygienic. However, the operation is not routinely recommended by British paediatricians, so you will need to consult your doctor if you wish to have this done.

Nappy changing

Whether you are using disposable or reusable nappies, or a combination of both, the method you use for nappy changing is basically the same. Start by getting everything you'll need together in one place.

Nappy rash

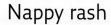

You need to change your baby frequently, otherwise he may get nappy rash – a red, sore rash in the nappy area. If he does develop a rash, there are specially formulated barrier creams that will soothe and heal it. Try to let your baby have some time each day kicking without a nappy on as the fresh air will help to keep his skin healthy. If the rash goes into the skin creases or up to the anus or vulva then thrush is more likely and an anti-fungal cream will need to be prescribed.

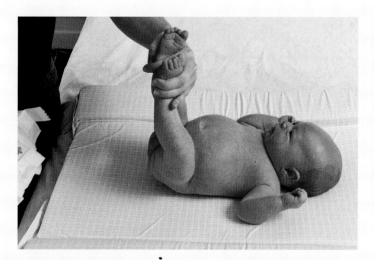

1 As you undo the dirty nappy, hold it loosely in place for a moment – your baby boy is likely to pee when he feels the cooler air on his skin. Use the old nappy to wipe away any soiling on his skin, gently holding his ankles together as you do so. Now clean his bottom, using plain warm water and cotton wool for the first six weeks. After that time baby lotion or a wipe can be used.

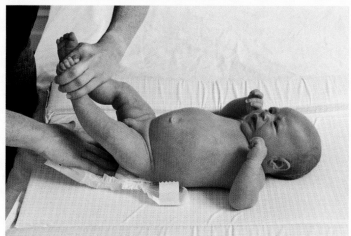

2 Make sure the whole nappy area is clean, and wipe his thighs and abdomen before patting the skin dry with cotton wool. You may want to apply a small amount of barrier cream before putting on a fresh nappy. Open up the clean nappy and, holding your baby by his ankles, slip the back of the nappy under him.

Equipment

Your changing equipment should include:

- a changing mat or towel
- a clean nappy (plus liner, pins and plastic cover if needed)
- baby lotion or wipes (if used)
- a bowl of warm water
- cotton wool
- barrier cream
- a nappy bag, or a bucket for reusable nappies
- a clean nappy, a vest and baby clothes.

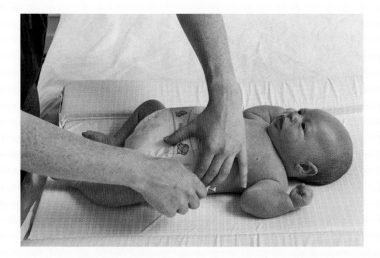

3 Now bring the front of the nappy up between his legs and fasten it in place, making sure that it's not too tight around the waist. If you are using a reusable nappy, add the outer wrapper cover before getting your baby dressed again.

Types of nappy

Disposables These work by drawing moisture away from the skin so that your baby's bottom is kept dry. They are convenient to use and are available in unisex styles in a wide range of sizes. You need to buy disposables that are the correct size for your baby's weight. Used disposables can be folded up and placed in a plastic bag before going into the bin. Alternatively, you can use a nappy wrapper that wraps and stores the nappies for several days so you can get rid of them in bulk.

Reusables Made of cloth or towelling, these nappies can be washed and reused. Some, such as the traditional terry towelling nappies, can be folded to fit babies of all sizes. Others are shaped and fit like disposables, so you may need to buy a bigger size as your baby grows. Both types need liners and waterproof covers. All-in-one nappies have an outer waterproof wrap attached to a shaped cloth nappy. Reusable nappies need to be rinsed, washed and dried after each use. You may wish to use a nappy laundry service which collects dirty nappies, replacing them with clean ones.

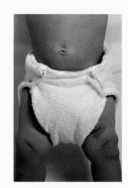

Week 4

Your baby's progress

Your baby is beginning to 'talk' and you will be able to hear her use different sounds to express her feelings. Make sure you repeat her coos and gurgles back to her to keep the conversation going. It's best to do this face-to-face so that she can watch your facial expressions during your 'chats'. She may start showing more obvious signs of recognition now and you may see her expression change when she sees you come into the room. Look out for her reactions when she sees you or your partner. You might notice that they are quite different from her reactions to other people.

You may also notice that your baby can maintain eye contact for longer now, and her eyes can track moving objects. Try attracting her attention with a colourful toy then watch as her eyes follow it as you move it from side to side. She may also be able to follow the object when it's moved up and down in front of her face, but her eyes won't follow it as smoothly.

During the first year your baby will learn a lot through watching and manipulating toys that offer different types of sensory stimulation. At this age black and white and strong bright colours will be more appealing than pastel shades, so choose toys in basic colours which offer a variety of different movements, sounds and textures. A baby-safe mirror will fascinate your baby as she studies her reflection. Try placing one in her crib where she can lie watching herself.

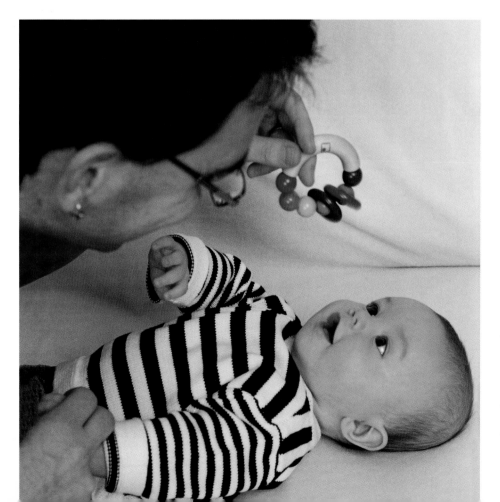

Playtime can be lots of fun for both you and your baby. Use colourful toys and objects to stimulate her senses.

Parents' survival guide

Mums

You are required by law to register your baby's birth within 42 days of the birth in England, Wales and Northern Ireland and within 21 days in Scotland. If you had your baby in hospital you may have been able to do this at the hospital before coming home. If you weren't, or you had a home birth, you will need to go to a register office to register the birth. Your midwife will be able to give you details of your local office, or you can find them in your phone book or on the website for your county council or metropolitan borough. You are not restricted to your local office, but it will take a few days longer to obtain the birth certificate if you go to one outside the district in which you live.

The registrar will want to know your baby's name and gender and the place, date and time of the birth. If you have had twins or more, you'll need to supply this information for each baby. The registrar will require your details and those of your partner if you are married.

Once the birth has been registered you'll be given a free short birth certificate which contains only your baby's details (you'll need this to claim child benefit) and a form to register your baby at your doctor's surgery. If you want a full version of the certificate that includes all your details as well there will be a small charge. You can buy further copies of both types of certificate at any time.

Dads

If you and your partner are married, either one of you can register the birth. If you're not married but you both want your name to appear on the certificate, you will need to go to the register office together. If for some reason you can't do this, you must sign a Declaration of Paternity which you can get from the registrar which your partner will need to take with her when she registers the birth.

Milestones for week 4

Your baby...

* may be able to hold her head up briefly when being supported against your shoulder
* can probably track with her eyes an object being moved from side to side
* may be able to keep her eyes on an object being moved vertically a little way
* will enjoy looking at herself in a mirror
* may show signs of recognition when you or your partner enter the room.

You...

* will probably be feeling more confident about the everyday babycare routines such as nappy changing and bathing your baby
* may have settled into some sort of routine with your baby
* can talk to your health visitor about any problems you may be having
* will notice that the period-like discharge you are having is lessening and may be turning from red to pinky-brown.

Colic

If at two to four weeks of age your baby has periods of prolonged crying, often at the end of the day and lasting into the evening, she may have colic. This describes a normally healthy, well-fed baby who, for no apparent reason, cries or screams for several hours at a time, often drawing up her knees as though in pain, and who cannot be comforted. Colic is a very distressing condition for babies and an equally wearing one for parents.

About 20 per cent of all babies develop colic, usually within the first month, and most get over it by about three months, although in some cases it can last longer. It occurs equally in boys and girls, and in first and subsequent children. The exact cause is not known, although there are a number of possible reasons, all of which are worth investigating if your baby suffers from this condition.

How can you help?

Helping a baby with colic

Things to do to soothe your baby:

❉ if you're breastfeeding, consider changing your diet as your baby may be reacting to your milk. Try cutting out spicy foods, wheat products, beans, broccoli, cabbage, caffeine and alcohol. After a few days reintroduce the foods, one at a time, allowing a few days between each. This should allow you to see if any are causing the problem. Milk products in your diet could also be a cause, but before you eliminate these you need to discuss your overall diet with your doctor or health visitor

❉ if you are bottle feeding it may help to change the type of formula you are giving, but always discuss any changes with your health visitor first. The amount of feeds offered – both too little and too much – could also be to blame

❉ colic could be a sign that your breastfed baby isn't getting enough hind milk, so allow her to suckle for as long as she wants at the breast

❉ you may have noticed that your baby passes a lot of wind during a feed and shows discomfort before and during a bowel movement. This may be because your baby's gastrointestinal system is still immature, so making sure that she is thoroughly winded both during and after each feed may help. If you're bottle feeding, use an anti-colic teat. There are a number of over-the-counter anti-colic remedies available, but not all health professionals believe that these are of any real benefit to a baby

❉ your baby may cry more because her central nervous system is still immature, making her tense and nervous. Letting her suck on your finger or a sterilised dummy may help to soothe her. Sometimes, swaddling or rocking a baby, or exposing her to 'white' noise, such as a washing machine or vacuum cleaner, can help. Baby massage is thought to help, especially when applied to the feet and tummy (*see* pp.128–9).

Things to do to help you:

❉ colic does no real harm to your baby, but it can put a lot of strain on you and your partner. If your baby's crying makes you feel tense and upset, put her down somewhere safe and walk away until you are feeling calmer. It may help you both to go out for a walk in the fresh air – the movement may soothe her and the exercise could make you feel better. If the colic occurs day after day, ask your partner or a friend to babysit for a short time during the colicky phase while you take a break

❉ try to remember that colic doesn't last for ever; in a few weeks it will probably stop as abruptly as it began. However, if you are really feeling under stress don't be afraid to ask your health visitor for help – she'll have heard it all before and won't think any the worse of you for finding it hard to cope.

Dummies

If your baby is soothed by sucking you may want to consider giving her a dummy. It is generally agreed that the moderate use of a dummy during the first year has no adverse effect on first teeth coming through. However, if you are breastfeeding it may be wise to wait until breastfeeding is well established, as sucking a dummy is a very different action to breastfeeding and swapping from one to the other does seem to confuse some babies.

Buy an orthodontic dummy, as these have been designed to be better for developing teeth. Dummies made from latex are softer and more flexible than silicone, but they don't last as long. You'll need several so you can switch them frequently and keep any spare ones sterilised (some come with holders to keep them clean when not in use). Make sure you inspect your baby's dummies regularly and throw them away at the first sign of wear.

You can stop your baby from becoming too dependent on a dummy by only letting her use it to help soothe her to sleep.

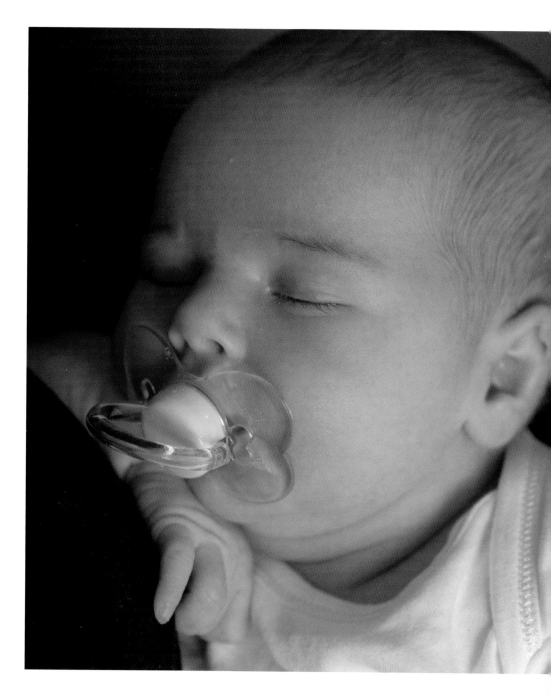

Crying

Your newborn baby has no other way of expressing how she is feeling other than by crying. She will cry for a number of reasons, such as being too hot, too cold, hungry, thirsty, tired or simply in need of a cuddle, and it's up to you to interpret what she's trying to tell you. It won't take you long to work out what her different cries mean. There is usually a whole world of difference between a tired 'I need to go to sleep' cry and a hungry 'I need to be fed now' cry.

If your baby's crying sounds unusual and differs from her normal cry, it could be a sign that she is unwell. Listen to your instinct and call a doctor if you are worried.

As your baby grows she will start to communicate with you in other ways such as by eye contact, cooing and making different noises, so it becomes easier for you to understand what she wants. By understanding her needs and responding to them you will be able to reduce the amount she cries. At around six weeks your baby is likely to begin to spend more time asleep at night and awake during the day, so her crying will probably become more specific – she needs changing or feeding, or she's bored and wants you to entertain her. She will also have found another means of communicating with you – smiling.

By the time your baby reaches four or five months old her crying should have reduced significantly. As she grows older and starts communicating with sounds and then words, she will often use crying only as a last resort.

Responding to your baby

Your response to your baby's cries and the way you comfort her can affect the bond that grows between you, especially during the first weeks of life when your baby may be finding the world outside the womb a strange and frightening place. By going to her as soon as she cries you will be showing her that you care and that you are there to protect and look after her. Of course she's too young to understand this now, but over time this early response will help to form the basis of a deep, loving relationship between you.

Don't ever worry that you are spoiling your newborn by picking her up when she cries; she isn't crying because she's being demanding or fussy, she's simply crying because she needs something and, by responding to her, you are answering this need. It's impossible to give your baby too much love – in fact, research has shown that babies whose needs are not met when they are tiny become more demanding as they grow, not less.

When your child is older and settled into a routine you will know when her cries are a sign of need and when she is just crying as a result of boredom, so you'll be able to respond accordingly. Leaving your older baby to cry for a short while won't do her any harm, and you may find that she settles herself.

Some babies just seem to cry a lot and nothing their parents do makes any difference. It is hard to live with an incessantly crying baby, and if you find yourself in this position you will need to develop strategies to help you cope (*see* Things to do to help you, p.42, and Crying cures, right). If none of these are effective you should talk to your health visitor or get in touch with Cry-sis (www.cry-sis.org.uk), a support group for parents who have problems with their baby's sleep and crying.

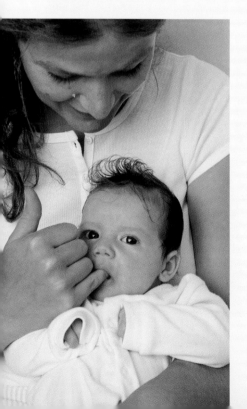

Instead of a dummy, allow your baby to suck your clean finger. It's a good way to pacify her if she is restless and tearful.

Crying cures

Before you try the following ploys, always check for the obvious reasons why your baby may be crying and look for any signs that she may be unwell. Once you are satisfied there is nothing wrong you could:

❀ sing to her
❀ put her in a baby sling so that she feels close to you
❀ walk or drive her round the block
❀ play music
❀ try the colic remedies on p.42
❀ offer a dummy.

Controlled crying

An approach that some parents have found helpful is controlled crying. This is a way of teaching your older baby to go to sleep on her own, so that if she does wake up in the night, she will be able to go back to sleep without your help. You could try this once your baby no longer needs a night feed but is still waking out of habit. You can do this during daytime naps as well.

❀ Settle your baby on her back in her cot when she is sleepy, but not asleep, and leave the room.
❀ If she cries, wait for five minutes before going back into the room.
❀ Don't pick her up, but reassure her by talking gently and stroking her, then leave the room again.
❀ If she continues to cry, wait another six to seven minutes and then go back in and reassure her.
❀ Gradually increase the time between return visits until she falls asleep.
❀ Repeat this routine over a number of nights until your baby learns that she can fall asleep on her own.

Week 5

Your baby's progress

Your baby is likely to have grown as much as 2.5 cm (1 in) since his birth and he will probably be putting on weight rapidly now. You may even notice that his first baby clothes are beginning to become too small for him.

As your baby gains more control of his movements you will see him attempt to reach out for things and he may even try to bat objects close to him with his hands. Although he is still not able to control his movements, these early lunges are his first attempts at hand-eye coordination. To encourage him, ensure that there are interesting toys positioned where he can reach them and help him to make contact with them by putting them into his grasp.

As his vision improves your baby will enjoy looking at new and interesting things. Carrying him around the house from room to room, pointing out different items as you go, will give endless entertainment. Watch him greet objects that he finds especially interesting,

perhaps the family dog or cat, with squeals of delight and excited waving of his arms and legs.

Your baby may also show obvious signs of delight at being with others, especially older brothers and sisters. However, you should watch out for signs of over-stimulation – after a while he may become restless and fretful. Remember that he has only been out of the dark, insulated womb for a few weeks, so he still needs periods of peace and quiet away from bright lights and loud noises.

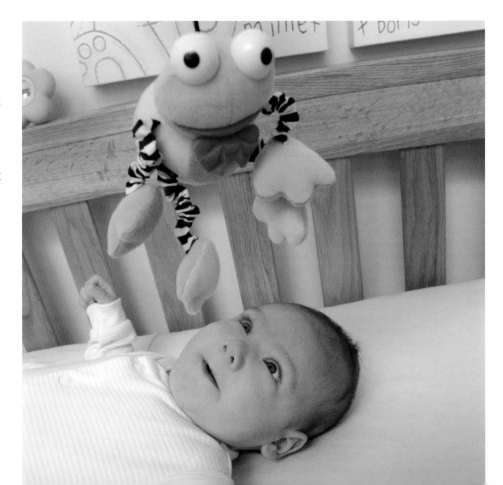

Try to place interesting objects and toys around your baby so that he can be stimulated if left on his own for a few minutes.

Parents' survival guide

Mums

You may have experienced an overwhelming surge of maternal love as soon as your baby was put into your arms, but you may have found that it has taken a few weeks for you to feel that you have properly bonded with your baby, which is natural, too.

Bonding is the intense attachment that develops between parent and child and makes you want to protect and love your child more than anything in the world. Although your baby is born with a deep-rooted psychological need to have close interaction with you, you may need to get used to him before you are able to experience this feeling. Very often parent-baby bonding develops gradually through everyday caring and nurturing and you find that, as you get to know him and learn how to soothe and comfort him, your feelings will deepen.

Bonding is a complicated process and parents can feel extremely guilty if it doesn't happen in the way they imagined it would. If you are struggling with your feelings for your baby, or are worried that you don't have the attachment for him that you think you should, talk to your doctor or health visitor. You may be suffering from postnatal depression which, left untreated, can seriously delay the bonding process.

Dads

Although there is a lot of emphasis put on mother and baby bonding, it's equally important for fathers to bond with their babies. This may happen at birth but more often takes a little time. You may not be as involved in day-to-day care as your partner, but there are many things you can do to develop a bond with your baby.

If your baby is being breastfed you obviously don't have the same opportunity as your partner to get close to him while he feeds (unless you are offering expressed milk in a bottle), but other than breastfeeding there is nothing else you can't do for your baby. Cuddling and talking to him and involving yourself in daily care routines will go a long way towards establishing that all-important father-baby relationship.

Milestones for week 5

Your baby...

✽ although still near-sighted, can see clearly up to a distance of about 30.5 cm (12 in)
✽ is beginning to gain control over his arm movements
✽ will be able to show enjoyment when he sees something he is interested in
✽ may smile when he sees you
✽ will probably enjoy sitting in a baby chair watching you while you do other things
✽ may be suffering from colic.

You...

✽ may be feeling the need to be with other adults. Ask your health visitor about postnatal classes or groups in your area
✽ may be struggling with a jealous sibling. Try to spend some time alone with your older child and offer plenty of reassurance
✽ are likely to be exhausted if your child is suffering from colic. Don't be afraid to ask for support from family and friends.

Bathing your baby

Your baby will usually need bathing only every other day at this age although, of course, if he enjoys it you can bath him more frequently. Choose a time when you are both feeling calm and relaxed, but not just after a feed or when your baby is tired and sleepy. Ensure the room is warm and that you have everything you need at hand before you begin.

You'll find it easiest to bathe a very young baby in a baby bath on a stand, or in one that fits into the big bath, as this will put your baby at a comfortable height for you to hold. Alternatively, you can use a washing-up bowl placed on something solid such as a table, or a 'tummy tub' which is specially designed to support your baby in an upright position. Before you undress your baby, fill the bath or bowl with about 10 cm (4 in) warm water, putting the cold in first and then mixing in the hot water. Test the temperature, using either a special bath thermometer (it should read 36 °C/96 °F) or the inside of your wrist or your elbow (the water should feel warm, not hot).

Once the bath is ready, undress your baby down to his nappy and clean his face and the folds of his neck (*see* Topping and tailing, pp.36–7). Now wrap your baby firmly in a towel and hold him so that his legs are under one arm and his head is supported by the hand of that arm. Holding him face-upwards over the bath, use your other hand to apply bath preparation or baby shampoo and wash

Equipment

You will need:
* a washing-up bowl or baby bath and stand
* a bowl of cooled boiled water (to wash face)
* a jug of warm water (to rinse hair)
* cotton wool
* a changing mat
* bath towels
* baby bath preparation
* shampoo (optional)
* a nappy
* clean clothes.

Safety note

Never leave your baby unattended in the bath, not even for a second. A baby can easily drown in as little as 5 cm (2 in) of water.

It can take a while to work out how to hold your baby in the bath so that you're both comfortable.

his hair, making sure that you keep the water and soap well away from his eyes. When you have finished, use a jug of clean water to rinse his hair, then pat his head dry with a towel.

Next, unwrap the towel and remove your baby's nappy, cleaning away any soiling. Lift your baby into the bath, supporting his head and back on your arm, while holding the baby's arm that's furthest away from you. Use the other hand to support your baby's legs and bottom as you place him in the bath and then to wash him with. When you've finished, lift him out of the bath onto a towel on your lap and wrap him up to keep him warm. Pat, rather than rub, your baby dry and then dress him.

Cutting nails

Although soft, your baby's nails can be sharp, so you'll need to keep them short to prevent him from scratching himself. The easiest way to do this in the first few weeks is to nibble the nails with your teeth or use an emery board to remove any sharp edges. As your baby gets bigger and his nails become stronger you'll need to cut them, either with nail scissors or clippers. You may find it easier to cut his nails when he's asleep, or when someone else is holding him. Always trim along the nail's natural line, being very careful and gentle so that there is no risk of catching his skin.

Ask someone to hold your baby steady while you cut his nails. This could make what might be a nerve-racking task a good deal easier.

Cradle cap

Also known as seborrhoeic eczema, cradle cap is the name given to yellowish scaly patches that may appear on a baby's scalp and, occasionally, on the eyebrows and behind the ears. Very rarely the condition spreads to the baby's body, when it can cause eczema in the nappy area. Cradle cap most commonly occurs from around four to five weeks through to one year. It can look unsightly but is harmless and won't cause your baby any distress. Small areas of the waxy crust may dry and flake off, leaving behind a red, inflamed area. Never be tempted to scratch or pick at the crust because this could lead to infection.

The cause of cradle cap isn't really known, although it could possibly be linked to hormonal changes which affect the oil-producing glands in your baby's skin.

No specific treatment is required for cradle cap as it will eventually clear up on its own. You may want to try massaging a small amount of olive or baby oil into your baby's scalp at night, which will help to soften the scales so that loose particles can be gently brushed off the scalp or combed out of your baby's hair the next morning. Once you've done this, washing your baby's hair with a mild baby shampoo will help to prevent any further build-up of scales. If the cradle cap becomes inflamed or infected, you will need to see your doctor, as antibiotic or anti-fungal cream may be required to treat it.

Overcoming breastfeeding problems

You may be breastfeeding without any problems now, but if you're still having difficulties, don't try to struggle on without help; ask your health visitor or a breastfeeding counsellor for advice. Breast problems can occur for a number of reasons, but they can usually be solved quite easily.

Blocked milk duct

This can happen if you have a build-up of milk, maybe as a result of the breast not being emptied because your baby isn't latching on properly, a missed feed or a restriction of the milk flow – for example, your nursing bra may be too tight.

Symptoms You will experience some tenderness and you'll probably see a red patch on the breast which may or may not feel hot. You may also find the breast is lumpy before a feed.

Treatment Apply a warm flannel to the area and massage the breast towards the nipple before feeding. Feed frequently, making sure your baby is latched on properly (see p.24). You can continue massaging the lump as your baby feeds and then use a breast pump to empty the breast completely once she's finished. If the duct doesn't clear you'll need to see your doctor or health visitor the same day.

Mastitis

This occurs when a blocked duct (see left) becomes inflamed. The inflamed area can often be found on the upper, outer part of the breast.

Symptoms The breast will feel hot and painful and the skin over the affected area is likely to be red and shiny. You may feel as though you have flu with a raised temperature and perhaps nausea.

Treatment Mastitis needs urgent medical treatment as, if left untreated, it can lead to a breast abscess. You'll also need to keep emptying your breast by offering your baby frequent feeds and using a breast pump. Taking an analgesic such as ibuprofen will reduce the inflammation and help with the pain.

Sore or cracked nipple

This is usually the result of your baby not being latched on properly (see p.24). She may be sucking on the nipple rather than taking a good mouthful of breast into her mouth.

Symptoms Your nipple will be red and you may experience a sharp shooting pain as your baby sucks.

Treatment Check your baby's position on the breast to make sure she's latched on correctly. If it really is too painful to feed, use a breast pump to express your milk so that you can give it to your baby in a bottle. Keeping your nipples dry between feeds will help. A calendula-based cream or a specially formulated antiseptic cream or spray will help to relieve the soreness.

Thrush

Sore nipples can also be a result of thrush (Candida albicans) on the nipple and in your baby's mouth. You are more likely to develop thrush if you suffered from it during pregnancy or if you or your baby have been on a course of antibiotics.

Symptoms Your nipples will be pink and shiny and you will experience shooting pains in the breast during and between feeds. Your baby may have white flecks in her mouth.

Treatment Both you and your baby will need an anti-fungal treatment to cure this, so you will need to see your doctor as soon as possible.

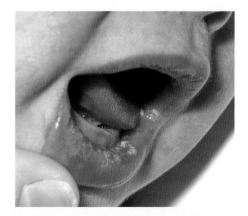

Oral thrush shows itself as white patches on your baby's tongue, cheeks, or the roof of her mouth.

It is important to keep breastfeeding, or at least to express milk at each feed so that your milk supply does not dry up.

Week 6

Your baby's progress

Your baby can now produce around four times the number of sounds she made as a newborn. She has learnt to imitate you by repeating many of the sounds that you make, especially vowel sounds. You can help increase her vocabulary by talking back to her and by gradually introducing more and more new sounds. Talk directly to her so that she can see your mouth as you speak.

Your baby is learning to anticipate routine activities and you may notice her react with excitement at feeding time or give you a welcoming smile as you greet her when she wakes in the morning. You can encourage her sense of anticipation by having regular routines that she can become familiar with.

Now that her neck muscles are growing stronger, your baby's head is less floppy. She may be able to hold it steady for a moment or two when she is held against your shoulder. If you lay her down on her tummy she may hold her head up for a few seconds in a more controlled manner than before. She may even be able to turn it so that she can look from side to side.

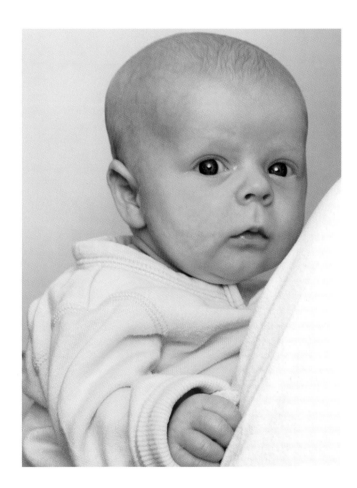

As your baby becomes stronger, she is visibly able to hold herself much more confidently. Her developing muscles are better able to support her body.

Your baby will probably smile back at anyone who smiles at her first, but she may be particularly responsive to her father now. The bonding process between father and child can take a little longer than the bonding between a mother and child if the mother is the main carer, but by this age your baby will have started to recognise you both as the special people in her life.

Parents' survival guide

Mums

Your postnatal check will take place around now, at your doctor's surgery, the hospital where you gave birth, or your own home. This check-up is designed to make sure that you are fit and healthy after the birth, so if you are worried about anything now is the time to discuss your concerns. It may help to make a note of any concerns that you want to mention, as it's easy to forget to ask a question when you are being given a lot of information.

During your postnatal check your doctor or midwife may weigh you, check your blood pressure and test a urine sample – it's a good idea to ask if you need to take one with you. You may also be offered an examination to see whether your stitches (if you had them) are healed and if your uterus has returned to its normal size. If you haven't had a cervical smear within the last three years an appointment will be made for one – usually around six months after delivery. If you're not immune to rubella (German measles) you'll be offered immunisation now. You'll be asked if you still have a vaginal discharge and whether you've had a normal period yet. Your doctor or midwife will need to know whether you have started having sex again and will want to discuss contraception with you. They'll also want to know how you are feeling emotionally, so be sure to tell them if you feel low, depressed or very tired all the time.

Dads

You have, no doubt, been told about postnatal groups which are run for new mothers. These groups offer your partner a chance to get to know other mothers in the area that will allow her to air and share any worries she has. However, postnatal groups are not just for mothers – there are now a growing number of fathers' support groups around which fulfil the same function, often run by fathers themselves. The health visitor should be able to tell you about any groups in your area, or you could ask other fathers. Alternatively, you could even consider setting up a new group yourself.

Milestones for week 6

Your baby...

- ✼ may be becoming more predictable about daily routines such as feeding and sleeping
- ✼ is likely to respond to you with a variety of different sounds
- ✼ probably sleeps for longer at night now
- ✼ reacts positively to her father's voice and face
- ✼ shows signs of becoming sensitive to her surroundings and will respond to different noises
- ✼ may have her first routine development check this week.

You...

- ✼ will have your postnatal check around now. This is a good time to discuss any issues that are concerning you
- ✼ may want to discuss contraception with your doctor
- ✼ may want to arrange some time for yourself, away from your baby. Ask someone you trust to babysit for an hour or so to give you a break.

Six-week check

Your baby will be offered a routine developmental check-up at six to eight weeks. This may be carried out by your doctor when you have your postnatal check, or you may be given a separate appointment at the baby clinic. This check-up is nothing to worry about – it's exactly what it says it is, a check-up to make sure your baby is fit and healthy. If you've been given a Personal Child Health Record book

Eight-month check

At some time between eight and nine months your baby will be offered another development check-up with your health visitor or doctor. This is simply to make sure that she is growing well and keeping healthy. Babies develop at their own pace, so you'll be asked questions about what your baby can do while the doctor or health visitor watches her. You may be asked to give her a toy so that the way she uses her hands (which demonstrates her fine motor skills) can be observed. Her eyes will be examined again to make sure that she doesn't have a squint or 'lazy' eye and she'll probably have a hearing assessment, known as a distraction-hearing test. Your baby's hips will be re-examined and if your baby is a boy you'll be asked whether there were any problems with his testes at his previous check-up.

Once again your baby will be weighed and measured and her head circumference checked. These measurements will be plotted on the growth charts in your baby's Personal Child Health Record book. The doctor or health visitor will want to know that your baby's immunizations are up to date and may discuss the measles, mumps rubella (MMR) immunisation which is due between 12 and 15 months.

Finally, other topics such as accident prevention and dental care may be discussed and you'll have the opportunity to raise any family issues you may want to talk about.

this will explain the different examinations your baby will be given and the findings will be recorded in the book before the end of the check-up.

At first the doctor will probably want to ask you about your baby. You may have already been asked to fill in a questionnaire in the record book, so do remember to take it with you as this will give the doctor a lot of the information he or she needs. If you are concerned that there may be a problem, now is a good time to talk about your worries.

Then your baby will need to be undressed so that she can be weighed. Her weight will be plotted on a chart (usually in the record book). The doctor will want to know how you are feeding her and if you are having any difficulties. You'll also be asked about her sleeping pattern and whether you are putting her down to sleep on her back (see Sleeping safely, p.30).

Your baby will then be examined from head to toe, just as she was at birth. Her head circumference will be measured and the results will be recorded on a growth chart. Her eyes will be examined with an ophthalmoscope and her mouth, ears and neck will also be checked. The doctor will feel the pulses in your baby's groin and listen to her heart with a stethoscope. Her tummy will be felt and her hips will be checked for any signs of dislocation. A boy's penis and scrotum will be examined to check that the testes have descended. Once your baby's hands and feet have been checked, her head control and limb tone will be tested before she is turned over so that the doctor can examine her spine and anus.

Your doctor should tell you what the tests are for as they are being done and what his findings are, but if there is anything you don't understand, don't be afraid to ask. If your doctor thinks that there might be a problem with your baby you will probably be referred to a paediatrician or specialist at the hospital to investigate the matter further. In many cases this referral is just a precautionary measure and no further action is needed.

Once the check-up has been completed you'll be asked to get your baby dressed again. The doctor may then talk to you about the immunisation programme which starts at eight weeks (*see* pp.66–7). If you have any concerns about the programme, this is a good time to discuss them.

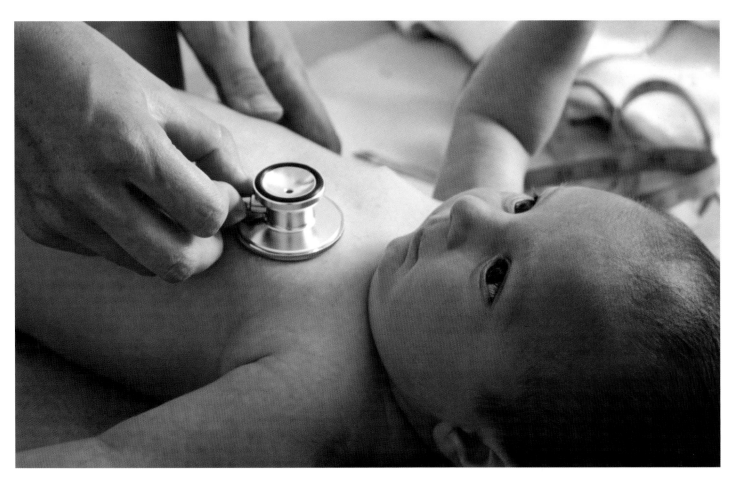

Regular checkups like the six-week check allow you to ask your doctor or health visitor about the things that worry you.

Week 7

Your baby's progress

Your baby's sight continues to develop so that she is now able to see clearly objects that are up to 50 cm (20 in) away. You may be able to see her try to focus when you move an object to the edge of her field of vision, though once it's out of her sight she'll lose interest in it. Although she will prefer looking at three-dimensional objects, she is also likely to enjoy brightly coloured pictures of things she recognises. Try showing her some pictures in a book and see how she responds.

Your baby is also getting better at identifying different sounds and may be starting to associate them with their source. Watch her reaction to your dog barking or the telephone ringing. She may enjoy music now, so try singing to her, or playing favourite CDs. She'll certainly enjoy it if you dance to them with her in your arms.

Playtime is taking on new dimensions for your baby, too. She will practise opening and shutting her hands and may even grip a toy if you place it in her open palm. She'll also enjoy sucking her hands and feet as well as playing with her fingers and toes and vigorously kicking her legs. All this activity is helping her learn that these body parts belong to her.

Your baby is probably becoming more sociable and will enjoy the company of others, as long as you are close by. Include her in your conversations when you are talking to friends and encourage other children to interact with her. She'll learn faster from children and will enjoy the company and stimulation she derives from them. Don't let her be overwhelmed, though – too many children or play that is too rough is likely to upset your baby, or even frighten her.

Board books with bright colours and pictures are the best books to read with your baby.

Parents' survival guide

Mums

Unless you are planning to become pregnant again almost immediately, you and your partner will need to decide what form of contraception to use. You may have already discussed your options when you had your postnatal check, otherwise you'll need to talk to your doctor, midwife, health visitor or practice nurse. Alternatively, if you prefer, you can go to your local family planning clinic.

If you're breastfeeding exclusively, your periods may not return until you start cutting down or cease feeding. However, this doesn't mean that you can't get pregnant, so don't use breastfeeding alone as a form of contraception.

You can usually start taking the pill from four weeks after the birth. The combined pill isn't recommended if you're breastfeeding so, unless you are bottle-feeding, you'd need to take the progestogen-only mini pill. Contraceptive injections and implants can be given from six weeks after the birth. If you want to conceive again fairly quickly, remember that it can take several months after you've stopped all these types of contraception for your fertility to get back to normal.

An intrauterine device (IUD) or system (IUS) can be fitted after six weeks, or eight if you had a Caesarean. If you used a diaphragm (cap) before it will need checking to make sure it still fits. Family planning by pinpointing your fertile days isn't reliable when you've just had a baby as it takes a while for your cycle to settle down.

Dads

Male condoms are the easiest form of contraception to use after childbirth, especially if your partner's periods haven't returned. Ovulation takes place approximately two weeks before a period, so your partner could become fertile without either of you realising it. Vaginal dryness is common after having a baby, so you may want to use a lubricant to prevent your partner feeling any discomfort. Any lubricant should be water-soluble so that it doesn't damage the condom.

Milestones for week 7

Your baby...

- ❈ can see almost twice the distance she could see as a newborn
- ❈ may be able to distinguish the source of familiar noises
- ❈ is able to express pleasure through smiles and even laughter
- ❈ enjoys being sociable
- ❈ is discovering that her hands and feet make great playthings.

You...

- ❈ may be finding it easier to get into a routine and stick to it
- ❈ will perhaps need to start to consider child care arrangements if you plan to go back to work at the end of your maternity leave
- ❈ are probably both looking and feeling a bit more like your pre-pregnancy self
- ❈ may want to treat yourself to a new outfit, or a visit to the hairdressers.

Your baby's temperature

Babies tend to have higher temperatures than older children and adults, so a baby's normal temperature can range from 36.5 °C (97.7 °C) to 37.8 °C (100 °F), depending on the time of day. His temperature will be lowest in the middle of the night and at its highest in the early evening. A baby won't usually be considered feverish until his temperature is over 37.8 °C (100 °F) in the morning and over 38.2 °C (101 °F) at night.

Your baby's body can't control his temperature in the same way as an older child's does, so it can rise and fall very quickly. He's also more sensitive to the surrounding temperature, so he can easily become overheated when it's warm and he's wearing too many clothes, or start to shiver because he isn't wearing enough. This is why you shouldn't just rely on a thermometer reading to know whether your child is ill or not. Some babies and young children can be ill with a normal or even below-normal temperature while others can have a slight fever and not be ill.

Your child's behaviour is the best guide to his health. If he's eating well and is responsive and contented there's less reason to worry if he has a temperature than if he is crying inconsolably, refusing food or appearing limp and unresponsive. If you are concerned about your baby always contact your doctor.

Thermometers

Thermometer strips, which are placed on the baby's forehead, are popular because they are inexpensive and easy to use. However, as they show the skin temperature rather than the body temperature they are not very accurate and should only be used as a guide.

Digital thermometers are a bit more accurate and can be used under the arm (and in the mouth for older children), although this means keeping your baby still while you hold the thermometer in his armpit for up to five minutes. Temperature readings from the armpit are about 0.5 °C (1 °F) lower than mouth temperature.

A more expensive but more accurate option is an ear thermometer, which measures infrared heat from the eardrum. This will give you a reading in seconds. However, it's important to follow the manufacturer's instructions carefully; this type of thermometer can give a low reading if it is not placed in the ear correctly. Another non-invasive type of thermometer is a forehead thermometer which provides an accurate reading by scanning the skin at your child's temple. This type of thermometer doesn't even have to touch the skin to produce the reading.

Safety note

The use of mercury thermometers is no longer recommended because of the problems of safely disposing of the mercury.

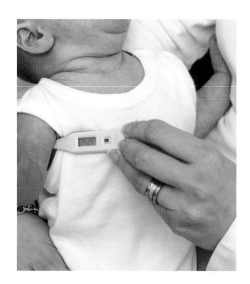

A digital thermometer held under the arm will give a reasonably accurate reading.

Giving medicine

It can be difficult to persuade your baby to take medication as the taste will be completely alien to her. At this age the only liquids she's probably ever tasted are breast milk or formula and perhaps water. Before giving any medication it's important to read the instructions and to make sure that the medicine is suitable for your child's age.

1 You may find it easiest to give your child medication by using a liquid medicine measurer resembling a syringe. Check the dosage and give the exact amount. If the medicine comes with a measurer supplied by the manufacturer, use this.

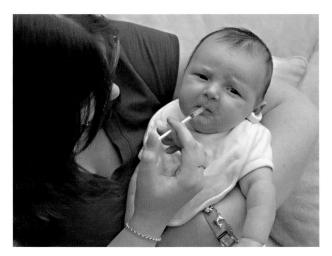

2 Sit your baby on your knee so that he's semi-upright and place the syringe or measurer in the corner of his mouth. Gently depress the plunger so that the medicine dribbles down his throat. Don't be tempted to rush this, as the medicine will be released too quickly and could choke your baby.

Pyloric stenosis

This is a condition that sometimes affects an otherwise healthy baby. It is more common in boys and symptoms usually appear two to three weeks after birth. Pyloric stenosis occurs when the muscular passage between the stomach and small bowel (pylorus) becomes narrower so that the inside of the passage closes up. This stops milk passing into the bowel to be digested. The symptoms include vomiting (often projectile), constipation and low or no weight gain. Apart from this your baby may appear bright, alert and extremely hungry, which can make the condition difficult to diagnose.

Initially you may be told that unsuitable nutrition is the cause and a change of formula or cessation of breastfeeding may be suggested. The vomiting, which occurs after every feed, can quickly lead to dehydration, so early diagnosis is important. Always seek medical help if your baby starts to vomit profusely or suffers from projectile vomiting.

A doctor can make a diagnosis by examining the abdomen for a lump. This is made easier if done after a feed, although a scan may be needed to confirm any findings. Treatment involves surgery, but it's a simple operation and the baby will recover very quickly afterwards with no ill effects.

When to call the doctor

The following signs could indicate that your baby is ill and requires medical attention:

* refusing feeds

* a fit or convulsion

* extreme drowsiness

* difficulty in breathing

* severe diarrhoea

* vomiting

* high fever

* an unusual rash

* crying uncontrollably.

Your baby could be unwell without displaying any of these symptoms, so you should trust your instincts. If you think your baby is ill, always contact your doctor. He or she may be able to give you advice over the telephone or fit you in without an appointment. If, for any reason, you can't get hold of your doctor and you're seriously concerned about your baby, then you should take him to the A&E department at the hospital. The staff there will be used to seeing young babies and, even if there is nothing seriously wrong, will be able to treat him and put your mind at rest.

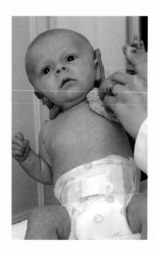

If your baby has a fever, sponge him down with some tepid water to reduce his temperature.

An electric fan, placed well out of reach of the crib, will help to reduce a fever and keep your baby comfortable.

Common ailments

Fever This is part of the body's defence mechanism against viruses or bacteria.
Symptoms A raised temperature, with or without other signs of illness (*see* left).
Treatment Help to lower his temperature by removing his clothes (apart from his nappy) and keeping the room well aired. A fan placed near the cot will help. Give plenty of fluids in the form of breast or formula milk. Cool your baby down by giving him a sponge bath with tepid water and then allow the water to evaporate off the skin rather than drying him with a towel. If your baby is more than three months old you can give him a dose of paracetamol suspension to bring down the temperature; paracetamol is not usually recommended for babies younger than this. Fever-soothing remedies will make your baby more comfortable, but always consult your doctor or health visitor before giving a young baby any medicine.

Febrile convulsions Also known as 'fever fits', these are usually triggered by a high temperature. They are relatively common and hardly ever serious.
Symptoms Jerky, uncontrollable movements and rolling eyes, or the child may turn blue and become rigid and staring. The 'fit' usually lasts for no longer than a minute or two.
Treatment Lie your baby down on his side to make sure he doesn't vomit and choke. Remove his clothing and sponge him down with tepid water. Try to remain calm so that

you are able to reassure him when it's over. If the fit doesn't stop, or your child hasn't fully recovered within half an hour, seek urgent medical attention by telephoning your doctor or calling an ambulance. Even if the attack is over quickly it's worth checking with your doctor in case he or she feels that further investigation is required. This is especially important if your baby is under six months.

Colds and coughs Colds are caused by airborne viruses and, because there are hundreds of different viruses, it's quite common for a child to have eight or more colds a year until he's built up his immunity. Most colds clear up within five to seven days.
Symptoms Blocked or runny nose, often accompanied by an irritating cough and possibly a fever.
Treatment Fever can be treated with the correct dose of paracetamol if your baby is three months or older. If stuffiness is hindering feeding, nasal decongestants may help but should be used for only two to three days. Saline drops can also help to relieve a stuffy nose. Offer your baby additional fluids and try raising the head of the cot (place books under the feet) so that your baby is tilted up, which will help him breathe more easily. A chesty cough could indicate an infection and antibiotics may be needed.

Ear infection This usually affects the middle ear and often accompanies a cold.
Symptoms Your baby may have a slight temperature and pull or rub his ear, which appears red; he may just cry a lot and seem generally unwell. Sometimes an ear infection causes diarrhoea.
Treatment An antibiotic may be prescribed, although most ear infections are caused by viruses and clear up on their own. Decongestant nose drops and, if your baby is old enough, paracetamol may be given to help relieve the pain.

Sticky eye This mild ailment is often due to the tear duct being partly blocked. It's not usually a problem after six months, but it can be recurring before then.
Symptoms The eyelashes are gummed together on waking and there may be pus in the inner corner of the eye.
Treatment Clean your baby's eyes twice a day with cotton wool dipped into cooled boiled water. Wipe from the inner corner outwards, using a fresh piece of cotton wool for each eye. If the sticky eye doesn't clear up within three days ask your doctor or health visitor for advice.

Conjunctivitis Also known as 'pink eye', conjunctivitis is an inflammation of the lining of the eye and eyelids. It can be caused by a virus or by bacteria.
Symptoms The eyelids may be gummed together with pus after sleep. The eye appears bloodshot and sore.
Treatment Antibiotic drops or ointment may be prescribed if the infection is bacterial. Viral conjunctivitis usually requires no treatment.

Diarrhoea The frequent passing of loose, watery stools may be caused by a virus or bacteria in the gut.
Symptoms The stools are more watery than usual, may appear greenish in colour and may smell different from usual. If diarrhoea causes dehydration, your baby will become lethargic and the eyes and fontanelles may be sunken.
Treatment Feed frequently and offer cooled boiled water between feeds. Be extra careful about hygiene and always wash your hands before attending to your baby. If the diarrhoea is severe and continues for more than 24 hours, seek medical advice. Your baby may need an oral rehydration mixture.

Vomiting Sometimes babies bring up unusually large quantities of feeds.
Symptoms Being frequently and violently sick, with or without other signs of illness.
Treatment A baby can lose a lot of fluid quickly when he's being sick frequently, so an oral rehydration mixture may be needed. Seek medical advice if your child is violently sick for more than 24 hours.

Week 8

Your baby's progress

Your baby has reached two months of age and, if you look back to how she was as a newborn, you'll be amazed at just how much she has learnt in such a short time. Physically she's a lot stronger and she's now gaining more control of her neck muscles. Although she can't hold her head steady yet, when you place her on her stomach she will probably lift up her head and may even try to raise her shoulders off the ground a little way in a mini push up.

Her vocal skills are developing fast. She is learning that her cries elicit a different response from you to her 'oohs' and 'aahs'. This realisation is another step on the way towards learning speech.

As a newborn your baby could track an item for only a few centimetres when it was moving horizontally in front of her. Now she can look from side to side and up and down, and will be able to follow an item moved across her field of vision.

Although she's been putting her hands in her mouth for a while, this was more a reflex action than a voluntary one. Now she deliberately uses her mouth to explore different tastes and textures which will help her to discover more about the world she lives in.

Your baby is also beginning to learn that things still exist when they are out of sight. She may fret when you leave the room because, to her mind, you have gone for ever, but when you reappear she'll be overjoyed. You can help reinforce this knowledge by showing her a toy, hiding it and then bringing it back into her view.

Chewing on toys, blankets and other objects is a natural instinct in your two-month-old baby and helps him learn about his fascinating environment.

Parents' survival guide

Mums

You and your partner may already be making love – some couples resume their sex life within the first month (though it's not advisable to have penetrative sex before two to three weeks). Alternatively, it could be that sex is the last thing on your mind right now. Whatever you are doing is right, for there are no fixed rules about when you should start making love after having a baby. The main thing is that you do it when it's right for you, and if that takes another month, or even longer, that's fine.

Looking after a baby is a 24-hour job, which is exhausting both physically and emotionally, so it's not surprising if the only interest that bed holds for you these days is sleep. But do talk to your partner about your feelings; it's easy for him to feel rejected if he wants sex and you don't. If you feel that you don't want to have sex, cuddling will help you remain close.

Although you should take things slowly and gently when you do start making love again, you shouldn't experience any pain or discomfort. If you do, it's important to talk to your doctor about it. Sometimes the way a tear or episiotomy has been stitched can cause long-term discomfort and another surgical procedure may be needed to put it right.

Dads

It's not only women who can suffer a loss of libido after childbirth – men, too, can go off sex after attending the birth of their baby. If this has happened to you, don't worry. It doesn't usually last for long and most men are soon eager to resume a healthy sex life, often long before their partners. Try to be patient and understanding if your partner seems more involved with the baby than she is with you. It's nothing personal; many new mothers are programmed this way, for the first few months at least.

Milestones for week 8

Your baby...

❋ may have her first immunisations this week

❋ is probably sleeping for longer stretches, although she may still be waking for feeds during the night

❋ is likely to be awake for longer periods during the day

❋ enjoys looking at and touching a wide variety of objects

❋ may be able to grab an object, but still can't let go.

You...

❋ will enjoy your baby's responsiveness when you feed, change or bathe her

❋ are likely to be confident about caring for your baby now

❋ may feel exhausted if you are still giving night feeds. Try to get some rest when your baby sleeps during the day

❋ can entertain your baby by showing her brightly coloured picture books.

Sibling rivalry

Some children take to their new brother or sister immediately with no obvious signs of jealousy. Others find the transition from only child to older child more difficult to cope with. If your toddler shows signs of jealousy towards your baby, try to remember that it's quite natural for her to resent the new arrival. Even if she seemed delighted with him at first, she may now be realising how much difference he has made to her life.

Try to imagine how your toddler must be feeling – all her short life she's been the centre of your attention but now she's having to share you with a demanding little stranger, and to make things worse, everyone else in her world is making a fuss of this new person in her life as well. Of course your toddler can't verbally express her feelings, in fact she probably doesn't really understand them, apart from perhaps wishing that the baby would go back to wherever he came from. The only way she can communicate her frustration and guarantee getting your attention is to misbehave, so be prepared for some pretty bad behaviour over the next few weeks.

Sometimes a toddler will regress so that she becomes more like the new baby, so you may find that she starts wetting herself, or demanding to go back into nappies even though she's been dry for months. She may be particularly difficult when you are breastfeeding and she may try poking or prodding the baby when you're not looking. In extreme cases she may even try to hurt the baby, so it's important to be constantly on your guard, never leaving your toddler alone with the baby.

It can be difficult for an older sibling when a new arrival takes attention away from her. Anticipate tantrums and jealousy and try to encourage her in her new role as big sister.

How can you help?

Toddler tactics

✿ If you can, involve your toddler in the care of your baby and remember to tell her repeatedly how clever she is, pointing out all the things she can do that the baby can't. Try suggesting ways in which she can help when you're bathing, feeding or dressing the baby and give her lots of praise when she does the things you've asked her to do. Don't force the issue, though – if she doesn't want to help, trying to make her do so will only create more resentment.

✿ Make sure you have some 'toddler time' together each day, without the baby, perhaps when he's having his morning or afternoon sleep. Make sure you give her your undivided attention and spend the time reading and playing games together. Talking to your toddler about how she feels and even sympathising with her feelings will help her to realise that you understand and that she's still very important to you.

✿ Babies love having other children around. When your baby is five to six weeks old he will enjoy watching your toddler's antics and will start to respond with smiles. If it hasn't happened before, this is likely to be the time when your toddler starts to forget about being jealous and begins to see her sibling as her new friend.

As your toddler becomes more used to the new baby, it is likely that signs of jealousy will dissipate. Be patient and keep your toddler involved in the baby's life.

Immunisation

Over the next few years your baby will be offered a series of immunisations against potentially serious diseases, starting with the five-in-one vaccine for diptheria, whooping cough (pertussis), tetanus, Hib and polio which is given at two, three and four months. Alongside the five-in-one your child will be offered an injection against pneumococcus at two months, meningitis C at three months and meningitis C and pnemococcus at four months. The latter immunisations are repeated at twelve months. They are followed by the MMR (measles, mumps and rubella) and pneumococcus immunisations at 13 months. If you're in a high-risk area, or there is a family history of TB (tuberculosis), your baby may also be offered immunisation against TB with a BCG vaccine, but this is no longer given as a routine immunisation.

When your baby is immunised she'll be given a weakened form of the disease (she won't get the illness from the vaccine) so that her body produces antibodies to it. If she then comes into contact with the disease she'll have the antibodies to fight it off. If, as happens very occasionally, she later catches the disease, it will be in such a mild form that it will do her no harm.

Immunisations are usually given intramuscularly in the thigh, using a small needle. You'll be asked to hold your baby close while keeping her leg still. Research has shown that allowing your baby to suck will reduce the pain that she feels, so you may want to put her to the breast. She'll probably cry for a few minutes after the injection and then settle. The injection site may become red afterwards and your baby may be a bit fretful and slightly feverish for 24 hours. Your health visitor may suggest that you give her liquid paracetamol, or Calpol, to soothe any discomfort.

Immunisation is a very important part of your baby's healthcare as it offers long-lasting protection against these diseases. If you are unsure about having your baby immunised, talk to your health visitor or doctor before making any firm decision against it.

You may automatically be sent an appointment for the immunisation programme, or you may have to book an appointment with your doctor or baby clinic. Your health visitor will be able to tell you what happens in your area.

When to call the doctor

After the immunisation you should seek immediate medical help if your baby:

❋ develops a temperature of 38 °C (100.4 °F)

❋ has a fit or convulsion

❋ cries in an unusual manner

❋ develops any other unusual symptoms.

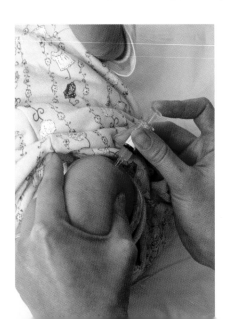

There has been controversy over certain immunisations in the past. Do discuss any questions you might have with your health visitor or doctor to reassure yourself if you are worried.

The diseases

Diphtheria This is a rare but potentially fatal disease in which a membrane forms at the back of the nose and throat, making it difficult, and sometimes almost impossible, for a child to breathe.

Hib Haemophilus influenzae type b is a serious disease that mainly affects babies and children up to the age of four. One form of the disease is Hib meningitis, which can cause brain damage, loss of hearing and other serious health problems.

Measles This is a serious illness which can cause encephalitis (inflammation of the brain) as well as convulsions, ear infections, bronchitis and pneumonia. Sometimes it is even fatal.

Meningitis C Group C meningococcal bacteria cause a form of meningitis and septicaemia.

Mumps Although this is usually a mild illness, it can have serious complications which affect both boys and girls and it may cause permanent deafness.

Pneumococcus This bacterium can cause a wide range of diseases from bronchitis and ear and sinus infections to life-threatening pneumonia, septicaemia and meningitis.

Polio The polio virus can cause muscular paralysis. Although rare in the UK, it can still be caught abroad. As the vaccine given is 'live' it's possible for it to be passed on through contact with your baby's nappy for some weeks after immunisation, so you'll need to check on your immunisation status before your baby has hers.

Rubella (German measles) Although it is a mild disease, it can harm an unborn baby if a woman catches it when she is pregnant.

TB (tuberculosis) This illness affects the lungs and can lead to TB meningitis.

Tetanus This disease affects the nervous system, causing painful muscle spasms. It is rare, but there is still a very real risk of contracting it and it can be fatal.

Whooping cough (pertussis) A highly infectious disease, it causes long bouts of coughing and choking. Bouts can occur as many as 50 times in 24 hours and the cough can last for up to three months. Whooping cough can cause convulsions, ear infections, pneumonia, bronchitis and even brain damage. In children under one year the disease can prove fatal.

For more information on childhood diseases *see* pp.108–11.

Baby blues and postnatal depression

During the first few days after the birth it's quite normal to experience the 'baby blues', a term used to describe irrational feelings of depression, weepiness and anxiety. These feelings usually last for a few days only and are thought to be caused by the large and rapid changes in hormone levels after childbirth.

If the feelings continue, or become worse, you may be suffering from postnatal depression (PND), a condition which affects at least one in ten women. Postnatal depression doesn't always follow on from the baby blues; although it most commonly occurs during the first two to four weeks after birth, in some women it doesn't appear until several months or even a year later. It can come on gradually or very quickly and can range from being relatively mild to very severe. At your postnatal check you may be asked to answer questions from the Edinburgh postnatal depression scale, a questionnaire especially designed to detect PND.

Postnatal depression is an illness that needs treatment just like any other, so if you suspect that you are suffering from PND don't struggle on without help. Talk to your health visitor or doctor so that they can advise you on the best way of coping with it. They will almost certainly recommend getting extra support and help with looking after your baby and they may also suggest counselling or perhaps meditation. In some cases of PND antidepressants are felt to be the best form of treatment, but do inform the doctor if you are breastfeeding as, in this case, not all drugs will be suitable for use.

Postnatal psychosis

This is a rare illness which affects around one in every 500 women after childbirth. Postnatal psychosis is most likely to affect you if you have a history of serious mental illness or there is a strong family history of it. Symptoms begin to appear from a couple of days to a couple of weeks after the birth. You may experience symptoms similar to PND along with some or all of the following:

❊ severe mood swings

❊ confusion

❊ delusions

❊ hearing voices

❊ seeing things that aren't there

❊ believing that you'll hurt your baby.

It's important to receive treatment as soon as possible. With the correct treatment – which could be in hospital – you should make a full recovery, although this may take some time.

The warning signs

Being aware of the symptoms of postnatal depression will help you and your partner to recognise the warning signs if they occur. The symptoms you need to look out for include:

❊ anxiety

❊ panic attacks

❊ feeling low, tearful and miserable for no reason

❊ irritability

❊ sleeplessness

❊ loss of appetite

❊ generally feeling unwell

❊ a loss of interest in the baby.

If postnatal depression is left untreated it can be difficult to appreciate the joy of motherhood during these first special weeks with your baby. Seek help and learn to enjoy spending time with your baby.

Week 9

Your baby's progress

Although your baby should always sleep on his back, vary his position during his waking hours by placing him in a baby chair, propping him up so that he is half sitting, and giving him plenty of tummy-time on the floor.

When he's on his front he may show early signs of crawling by raising his bottom in the air and trying to push with his feet. He may even manage to inch his way across the floor, when he may sometimes inadvertently roll onto his side and from there onto his back. He'll need your help to return to his front but, as soon as he has, he'll probably try doing it all again.

Your baby's memory is developing and he may now be able to remember things that capture his attention. Try squeezing a squeaky toy, then place it in your baby's hand and squeeze it again. If he's interested he'll want to squeeze it himself because he will have remembered the noise that it made. This type of game will also help your baby learn about cause and effect.

Your baby's attachment to you can mean that he feels lonely when you leave him, even for a few moments. He'll demand your attention by crying or fussing as he looks for you. Try talking to your baby as you leave the room so that he can hear you, even though he can't see you. This should comfort and reassure him.

Your baby is becoming more mobile and may be able to roll onto her side or her back without any help from you.

Parents' survival guide

Mums

If you've been the one getting up in the night for the past eight weeks, you are bound to feel tired; whether you are breastfeeding or bottle feeding, night feeds are exhausting. Sharing the load would certainly make life easier.

It may be that your partner works long hours and it doesn't seem fair for him to have to get up in the night, but sometimes finding a compromise that allows you both to get some rest is the answer. If you are breastfeeding you may feel there isn't much point in you both being disturbed, but there's no reason why you can't try expressing milk so that your partner can give the late evening bottle while you get several hours of sleep before the night feed. Your health visitor will probably advise you not to feed your baby expressed milk until he is four weeks old as there can be a problem with nipple confusion, but after this, once breastfeeding is well-established, there is no reason why you shouldn't express your milk. If you're bottle feeding, following the routine above shouldn't be a problem at all.

At weekends you could take turns, so that one of you has a complete night's sleep while the other sees to the baby. You'll be amazed at how refreshed you feel after just one undisturbed night.

Dads

Night feeds are tiring but they have one very big advantage – you get your baby all to yourself. There's something very peaceful about being alone with your baby in the middle of the night. If your partner is breastfeeding and doesn't want to express her milk, there are other things you can do to help during the night: you can be the one to get up to bring the baby into bed so that your partner can feed him; you can wind him during and after the feed and change him before putting him back in his cot. All these activities will not only help you bond with your baby but will also give your partner a much-needed break.

Milestones for week 9

Your baby...

* will attempt to grasp objects by swiping at them
* may try to reach out and grasp items on a baby gym or activity centre
* may be able to roll from his side to his back
* is likely to gurgle, blow bubbles and make raspberries as he practises his sounds
* gains stimulation from interacting with toys and people.

You...

* may be feeling desperate for some 'me' time. Get someone you trust to look after your baby for an hour while you have a bath, pamper yourself or simply read a book
* if you haven't taken up exercise yet, you may want to think about joining a gym which has a crèche
* may want to share night feeds with your partner.

Baby clothes

Most baby clothes are sized by the approximate age and weight or height of the baby. You probably won't require too many newborn clothes as your baby will grow into the next size within a matter of weeks – indeed, some babies are big enough to go straight into second-size clothes at birth. If your baby was premature you'll find there are plenty of clothes available to fit him, from really tiny outfits to smaller versions of newborn clothes. Prem clothes are usually sized by a baby's weight.

The important thing to remember with any first clothes is to keep them simple. Dressing and undressing your baby is likely to be stressful enough without having to worry about complicated fastenings, buttons and bows, so choose baby clothes that you can get on and off with the minimum of fuss. Look for vests made from soft, stretchy cotton fabrics with wide envelope necks that can easily be slipped over your baby's head. All-in-

one vests, which fasten between the legs, will prevent your baby from getting cold round the middle and are ideal if you dress your baby in separates. Stretch suits with poppers or zips from the neck to the crotch and down the legs are easy to put on and will allow you to change your baby's nappy without having to completely undress him.

As your baby grows and becomes used to being dressed and undressed, separates are the easiest replacement for stretch suits. It's best to save clothes such as pretty dresses, lacy cardigans, jeans and jackets for best as they're not really practical for everyday wear. Always make sure that the clothes you buy are made from easy-care natural fabrics that will wash and wear well. The care label will tell you whether the garment needs special treatment such as hand-washing, which you'll definitely want to avoid.

In warm weather your baby should be dressed in clothes that will keep him comfortably cool, with a sun hat for when you are out and about. On cold days you'll need outerwear that's roomy enough to fit easily over your baby's normal clothes.

Your baby's toes should never be restricted, so you'll need to keep a check on stretch suits, tights, socks and bootees to make sure that there is plenty of room for your baby's delicate feet. Although your baby won't need proper shoes until he starts walking and his feet need protection from hard surfaces, you may want to put him in soft shoes before this. These should always be made from a lightweight, breathable material such as cloth or soft leather and they should be flexible enough for you to be able to feel all his toes through them.

All-in-one stretch suits are ideal for a baby. They are easy to put on and to take off when your baby needs changing.

Dressing your baby

You'll find it simpler to dress your baby on a flat
surface so that you have both your hands free.

 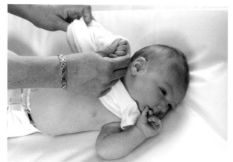 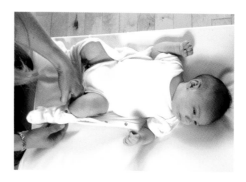

1 Using both hands, concertina the fabric of the vest. Then stretch the opening of the neck as wide as possible and draw the vest over your baby's head and face, taking care not to scrape his nose or ears. Straighten the fabric round his neck.

2 Gather up the sleeve in one hand and insert your other hand through the armhole so that you can gently guide your baby's arm through the opening. Do the same with the other arm. Pull the vest down and fasten the poppers between your baby's legs.

3 Now, lay the stretch suit out flat and lay your baby on top of it. Gather up the fabric of one leg and slide his foot into it. Pull the fabric up his leg, then repeat with the other leg.

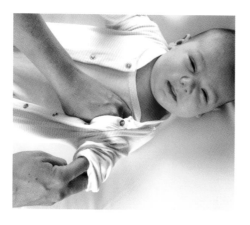

4 Gather up the sleeve fabric and gently guide it over your baby's wrist. Slide the sleeve up his arm and over his shoulder, then do the same with the other arm. Adjust the stretch suit so that the two sides line up and then, starting at the crotch, do up the poppers.

Baby essentials

Your baby's first wardrobe doesn't need to be extensive or complicated. Here are the essential items it should include:

❈ six stretchsuits (long-sleeved)
❈ six vests (short-sleeved)
❈ two or three cardigans or jackets
❈ shawl or snowsuit (for winter)
❈ mat, mittens and bootees or socks (for winter)
❈ sunhat (for summer).

Week 10

Your baby's progress

Grasping is now becoming a voluntary action for your baby rather than a primary reflex. Watch how he tries to make contact with an object and then, once you've placed it in his grasp, holds on to it tightly. He'll move it around, keeping it in his field of vision, and will bring his other hand up to help hold the toy while he explores it with his mouth. He hasn't learnt how to control his grasp, so when he's finished with a toy he simply lets it drop out of his hands.

At this age your baby has no concept of depth perception, so he doesn't know when objects are close or far away, but he's beginning to learn. Try moving a toy close to his face – when it gets too near he'll probably blink. If you draw his attention to an object placed just out of his reach he may make a lunge for it, even though he won't always manage to make contact.

Your baby's vocabulary continues to grow and he may enjoy spending time lying in his cot talking to himself. He will love having 'chats' with you and you may notice him trying to imitate any new sounds he picks up from your

conversations. His listening skills are also improving and he may start to vocalise recognition of familiar sounds.

His neck is a lot stronger now and he can hold his head steady when he is upright. He may be able to lift his head as much as 90 degrees when he's lying on his front. You may notice your baby is constantly on the go, kicking his legs and waving his arms around. These movements are smoother and more refined now, showing little trace of his jerky newborn actions.

Try playing peek-a-boo with your ten-week old and see how much he enjoys mimicking your vocal patterns and watching your face appear from behind your hands.

Parents' survival guide

Mums

By now you're probably a regular at your local child health clinic. This may be attached to your doctor's surgery or located in a church hall or similar building. Wherever it is situated, it's run by health visitors and doctors who are there to help and advise parents on any problems they may be having with their babies. You'll no doubt have found it a useful place to obtain information and to meet other mums, specially if there is a parent and baby group held there each week. These weekly get-togethers can be a great way to make new friends.

If your clinic also sells second-hand baby equipment and clothes, or has a board where the equipment can be advertised, this can be a good place to buy and sell 'almost new' baby items.

Dads

Don't think that child health clinics are just the domain of mums with babies and young children – there's no reason why dads can't attend clinic appointments, or even bring their babies along to be weighed. You may have already met your health visitor on her first visit to your home, but if you didn't and you're worried about going, why not accompany your partner on her next visit so that you can see how dad-friendly the clinic is? Your partner will certainly appreciate your support when she has to take your baby for his immunisations. Mums can often be more upset by these than the babies are.

Milestones for week 10

Your baby...

* will enjoy holding things that give him the opportunity to explore different shapes and textures
* loves entertaining you with new noises, bubble blowing and gargling
* uses his arms and legs to express his excitement
* finds simple games such as peek-a-boo great fun.

You...

* probably feel more in control of your life now
* may have adjusted emotionally to being a mum
* are perhaps being more adventurous in your outings with your baby.

Pets and babies

Most cats and dogs who are well established as family pets are pretty tolerant of babies, provided their lives are not completely disrupted by their arrival. The key to this is to train your pet in advance by setting clear boundaries. For example, don't allow your dog to go upstairs or your cat to go in the room where your baby will be sleeping. Your cat should never be allowed in your baby's cot or Moses basket either, but just in case it manages to sneak into the room, a cat net is an essential piece of equipment so that there's no risk of your cat sitting on your baby's face and suffocating him. Do make sure that the cat net is fastened properly, otherwise it will just act as a cradle for the cat and won't offer your baby the protection that is needed.

When you bring your baby home from the hospital or birthing centre for the first time, make a fuss of your pet before introducing it to your baby. Allow your baby and pet to spend time together in the same room over a period of days so that they both get used to each other, but never leave your baby alone with your pet.

At first your baby won't take much notice of your pet so it should be relatively easy to keep them apart, but he will soon want it to be his playmate. It is not likely that a well-trained pet will deliberately hurt your baby, but it is a possibility – especially if he hurts it, when it might instinctively retaliate by biting or scratching. So it's important, too, to give your pet a safe place such as a utility room that it knows it can escape to once your child starts crawling and walking.

Generally, provided your pets are clean and healthy and have been wormed and treated for fleas, they can become constant loving companions for your child.

Safety note

For the sake of good hygiene your pet should never be allowed to lick your baby's face and hands. Animal food dishes and litter trays should be kept out of your baby's reach.

It is important to give pets a safe place where they can escape from a baby's unwanted attention.

Fresh air and exercise

With or without a dog, a daily walk in the park or the countryside is an ideal way of getting some exercise and giving your baby a good dose of fresh air, too. A brisk walk will give you an energy boost while the movement of the buggy or sling will probably lull your child to sleep. So, making time to take your baby out for a walk each day makes good sense and, as he gets older, he will start to notice and enjoy the new sights and sounds that you encounter on your walks together. It won't be too long before he's looking forward to trips to the park, perhaps to the baby swings, or to feed the ducks.

Fresh air can help your baby in other ways, too. When it's warm, allowing him to spend time outdoors without a nappy on so that the air gets to his bottom will help to keep his skin clear of nappy rash. Drying washable nappies and your baby's towels in the fresh air will keep them soft so that they are gentle on his skin.

Protect your baby from the sun with a parasol and use a fine mesh net to keep insects away and to prevent any wandering cats from getting into the pram.

Take your baby for a brisk walk every day, to the park or even just around the block. It will energise you and refresh you both.

Week 11

Your baby's progress

Your baby will probably be capable of sitting up now, although she will require some help from you. If you support her back you'll see that her neck is now strong enough to hold up her head, and that she will be able to hold it steady for short periods of time. She'll enjoy seeing the world from this new position, so try sitting her in a baby chair so that she can watch you as you do things about the house. She'll still need plenty of tummy time, too, and you can encourage her to lift up her head and look around from this position by holding a toy somewhere near her that forces her to raise her head in order to see it.

By now, your baby's grasping skills are developing well, and you will notice how she grabs things using her whole hands – her finger control will develop later. She still won't have mastered the art of letting go of objects but you can help her by gently rubbing her fingers, which will encourage her to release whatever she is holding.

Your baby sleeps for longer periods now, although she may still be waking in the night and early in the morning. Instead of rushing to pick her up, try leaving her for a few minutes to see if she settles herself.

By now your baby can show a range of feelings and reacts to your emotions, too. If you are sad your baby will become upset; if you're laughing she may join in too. As you become more in tune with each other's emotions you create the foundation for her social reactions.

Lay your baby on his stomach and encourage him to look up at objects. This helps him to work those ever-strengthening neck muscles.

Parents' survival guide

Mums

All mothers (or the person responsible for looking after a child) in the United Kingdom are entitled to claim Child Benefit. This is a tax-free sum of money the government pays you regularly for each of your children, from their birth until they are at least 16 years of age. If you haven't started claiming, you should do so now – you'll lose some of the money you are entitled to if you don't claim within the first three months of your baby's life.

You may have been given a claim pack before you left the hospital. If not you can get one from your local Jobcentre Plus or Post Office, apply online at www.inlandrevenue.gov.uk/childbenefit, or call 0845 601 8040 and ask for a pack to be sent to you. You'll need to fill in the forms and send them to the Child Benefit Centre along with your baby's birth certificate, which will be returned to you.

The money will be paid into your bank, building society or Post Office account every four weeks (in arrears), unless you specifically ask for it to be paid weekly.

If you've decided to stay at home to look after your child, claiming Child Benefit can help to protect your state pension as it will qualify you for the Home Responsibilities Protection (HRP) scheme. HRP reduces the number of 'qualifying years' you must accumulate to receive the basic state pension, and you are automatically entitled to it for each full tax year if you are being paid Child Benefit for a child under the age of 16.

Dads

Once you or your partner have registered for Child Benefit you should be sent an information pack about the Child Trust Fund, along with a voucher worth at least £250 from the government. This is a long-term savings and investment account set up for children who are UK citizens and resident in this country. The idea is that the account grows over the years into a lump sum for your child to use at 18.

Milestones for week 11

Your baby...

* can probably support her head and upper back when she is helped to sit up
* may be sleeping for longer periods at night
* will enjoy sitting in a baby chair or pram so that she sees the world from a new position
* can show a range of different emotions.

You...

* may not have lost all your 'baby weight' and so want to go on a diet. Joining a slimming club could be the way to lose weight and make new friends
* will be confident about reading your baby's body language and facial expressions
* might enjoy a parent and baby group where you can meet other mothers with babies of similar ages.

Bedtime routine

Babies like routine, because it means they can anticipate what's going to happen next. By introducing a soothing, peaceful evening routine before bed you'll be helping your baby to recognise her bedtime and the need to sleep. It's good to start this from an early age if you can, but often the first weeks with a new baby are a bit chaotic and trying to impose any sort of routine may be impossible. If you haven't already created a bedtime routine, now is a good time to begin.

Make the last half hour before bed as peaceful as possible, so that your baby isn't over-stimulated and then too excited to settle. It can be difficult if this is the time when your partner comes in from work ready for fun with her. Instead of playing boisterous games, perhaps your partner could be the one to read or sing to her once she's settled in her cot.

You may want to start your routine with a bath, and you'll certainly want to feed and change her before giving her a cuddle and putting her down in her cot to sleep. If you can, put your baby down awake so that she learns to fall asleep on her own without being rocked or cuddled. Once she's accustomed to getting herself off to sleep there's more chance of her settling herself if she wakes during the night, otherwise she'll expect you to rock her back to sleep whenever she wakes. Read her a short story – although she won't understand what you are saying she'll enjoy the sound of your voice – or sing to her. Then kiss her good night and leave the room. She'll probably cry once she realises you've gone, but wait a few minutes before you go back in to her; if she's drowsy enough she may go to asleep.

Some babies don't like the dark, so you may want to leave on a night light which gives a comforting glow. This can be useful when you go in to check on her, too, as you won't need to disturb her by turning on the main light.

The room where your baby sleeps should be warm – around 18 °C (65 °F) – so that she doesn't wake up cold in the night. Put her down in a vest, nappy and stretch suit and cover her

Help your baby to relax before bedtime by making the last half hour before bed as peaceful as possible. Talk quietly and stroke and kiss your baby to soothe her.

with a sheet and several blankets, unless you're using a baby sleeping bag, in which case you only need a blanket or two. It's important that babies don't become overheated (*see* Sleeping safely, p.30), so check her body warmth by feeling her tummy or the back of her neck and adjust her bedding if need be. She should feel about the same temperature as you.

Your baby needs to learn to associate her cot with sleep, so even if you're putting her down for a nap during the day, draw the curtains. As she grows older you may want to introduce cot toys that will amuse her before she goes to sleep or when she wakes early in the morning.

Night feeds

If your baby needs feeding during the night you must persuade her that this is not a time for being sociable, so:

* keep the lights dim
* talk in a hushed whisper
* don't play with her
* change her with the minimum of fuss
* put her back in her cot as soon as she's finished feeding.

Sleeping

By now your baby is likely to be sleeping more at night and less during the day. You may still be feeding her at night, but not as often as when she was only a few weeks old. As she continues to grow you should find that her need for night feeds become less frequent and that she sleeps for longer periods.

Some babies don't settle at all well at night, and their parents become desperate through lack of sleep. If this is you, talk to your health visitor, who will be able to put you in touch with a sleep clinic. These are usually run by health visitors who have had special training in the management of sleep problems and who will be able to give you the help and support you are looking for.

Some babies make it very obvious when they are feeling sleepy and are ready for a nap.

Playtime

Through play, your baby learns to develop a lot of the basic skills she'll need as she gets older. During the first months, play helps her develop hand-eye coordination, encourages her manipulative skills and teaches her about cause and effect. As her play becomes more creative she will be developing self-awareness and imagination, as well as learning how to work things out for herself.

A newborn needs plenty of sensory experiences such as touch and sound in order to develop her senses further. Although toys will stimulate your baby's interest at each stage of her development,

for your newborn you are the best toy she could have. She'll learn more from watching your face and listening to the sound of your voice than she will from any toy you give her.

As well as liking to look at faces, your newborn is attracted to bright primary colours and the sharp contrast of black and white patterns. She prefers objects that move slowly, so a mobile hung over the cot and a mirror attached to the side so that she can see herself make good first toys. Babies tend to look to the right 80 per cent of the time, so make sure you put the mirror in her line of vision.

As your baby's visual perception develops she'll show a preference for increasingly complex patterns and will start tracking objects with her eyes. A simple first game is to attract her attention to an object and then try to get her to watch it as you slowly move it from side to side.

A baby's hearing is quite well developed at birth and during the first few months she will spend her time learning how to locate the source of the things she hears. You can help by playing a sound-tracking game using bells or rattles – babies are more sensitive to high-pitched sounds. Start by getting her attention, then move the bell or rattle to one side and then the other to see whether your baby makes any movement in the direction of the noise. Don't worry if she doesn't at first; it will take her a while to learn this skill.

Later your baby will enjoy exploring new textures and sounds herself. Rattles and toys made from various materials will help her learn about sound and touch. As she becomes stronger and her movements are more controlled she will reach out for things to hold and will start to experience the difference between light and heavy, soft and hard.

Using a toy as the main point to a game helps your baby to learn about sharing the focus of attention and will encourage

Toys for early learning

Any toys you give your baby should be appropriate to her age. Toys for older children will be too complicated for her and may have small parts that could be dangerous as she could choke on them. Toys that are too young will quickly become boring and will lack any challenge for her.

0-3 months
- Mobile.
- Wind chimes.
- Unbreakable mirrors.
- High contrasting mobiles.
- Brightly coloured cloth or board books.
- Simple, tactile and chewable toys.
- Baby play gyms/play mats.

3-6 months
- Spinning tops.
- Rattles.
- Squeaky toys.
- Colourful teethers.
- Toys with different textures.
- Cot toys.
- An activity centre.

her development of language and communication skills. Although she will probably show great interest in the toys you play with together, at this age it's because she's enjoying the play rather than the toys. For her, toys are only an accompaniment to the play itself.

Traditional games

During these first months your baby will enjoy turn-taking games such as 'peek-a-boo', bouncing games such as 'This is the way the farmer rides' and games that involve touching and tickling, for example 'Round and round the garden' and 'Incey, wincey spider'. Once she's gained head control she'll probably delight in games that involve more rough and tumble such as 'flying', where she's lifted into the air above your head and back down again.

Always be guided by your baby when it comes to playtime. Some days she may want to play games which include lots of interaction and stimulation, on others she may be happier sitting having a cuddle while you look at a book together.

Your baby will enjoy looking at herself in a mirror as she becomes more self-aware.

Week 12

Your baby's progress

You've reached the three-month mark and your baby is developing fast. He now reacts to familiar situations by smiling, cooing and making excited movements. Watch his reactions when he recognises preparations for a feed, a bath or going out.

Physically your baby is a lot more mobile than he was a month ago and his movements are smoother and more continuous. He can bring his hands from his sides to meet in front of him and he can kick his legs vigorously, both alternately and together. When he's lying on his tummy he may be able to lift up his head and upper body, using his forearms for support. He's also likely to be making swimming motions with his arms and legs. This is his pre-crawling stage, where he practises the skills he will need later. He'll be practising rolling over, too, and can probably roll from back to side now, and vice versa.

Although he smiles a lot now, he may have started to be more selective about who gets the biggest smiles. These will probably be reserved for those he knows best, while strangers may be greeted with a curious stare. These early signs of independence don't mean that he has less need of physical contact with you. Holding, cuddling and touching will always play an important part in your baby's development and wellbeing.

Your baby's vocabulary has increased and goes on increasing as he listens to and tries to copy the many different noises he hears around him in his environment. You'll hear lots of vowel sounds as these are the easiest for him to make, and they will probably be accompanied by a variety of grunts, gurgles and squeals.

Your baby will be using her hands more, bringing them to meet in front of her and opening and closing the fingers.

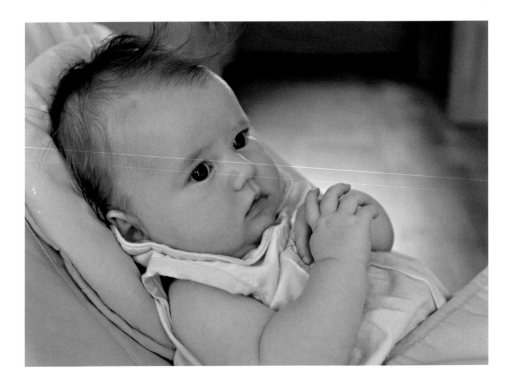

Parents' survival guide

Mums

You'll be looking and feeling a lot more like your pre-pregnancy self now, but that doesn't mean that you should stop doing those all-important pelvic floor exercises (sometimes referred to as Kegel exercises); you should still be practising them several times a day. In fact, you should continue to exercise these muscles for the rest of your life.

Your pelvic floor muscles hold the bladder, uterus (womb) and bowels in place. They are often stretched and weakened during pregnancy and, although by now (if you've been exercising them frequently) they should be stronger, it's worth giving them a good squeeze every day. If the muscles are allowed to remain weak you may find that you suffer from stress incontinence (when small amounts of urine leak out when you cough or laugh) and that intercourse is less enjoyable.

To exercise the pelvic floor muscles, squeeze and lift them as though you are trying to stop the flow of urine when you go to the lavatory. You can do this anywhere – while you're washing up, standing in the queue at the supermarket checkout or feeding your baby. Do them several times a day in batches of ten.

Dads

If you're out at work all day it can be very tempting to play with your baby as soon as you come home. However, if your arrival coincides with the period just before your baby's bedtime, you'll find that too much excitement will over-stimulate him, making it much harder to get him to settle when you put him down to sleep. Try to spend the time before bed doing quiet things with your baby such as reading or talking quietly to him and save the more energetic play for when you're together during the day.

Milestones for week 12

Your baby...

❀ will be due for his next series of immunisations soon
❀ may open and close his fingers and bring his hands together
❀ could stop waking for a night feed
❀ may show signs of being shy of strangers.

You...

❀ may need to start thinking about returning to work
❀ could consider expressing milk so your partner can give you a break from feeding
❀ could be finding life easier as your baby starts to amuse himself for short periods.

Expressing milk

Once breastfeeding is well established you may want to express milk occasionally so that you can leave your baby in someone else's care while you go out. You can express milk by hand or you may choose to use a manual or electric breast pump. Both types work by drawing the milk through your nipple into a sterilised container – either a bottle or a special poly bag ready for freezing. Hand pumps are cheap, portable and quiet, but they can be quite hard work if you want to express milk frequently. Battery or electric pumps are much quicker, but they are quite noisy and a lot more expensive. The Association for Breastfeeding Mothers, La Leche League and the National Childbirth Trust (NCT) all hire out breast pumps, or you may be able to hire one through your local health authority. Your health visitor will be able to tell you whether you can do this in your neighbourhood.

When and how you express your breast milk is up to you. You may want to experiment to find out what suits you best. For example, if your baby only feeds from one breast at a time, you could express from the breast he hasn't fed from. If he feeds from both breasts but doesn't empty the second one you could express the milk that's left. Maybe your baby goes for three to four hours between feeds, in which case you could try expressing midway through this period.

Expressed milk should be kept for no more than 24 hours in the coldest part of the refrigerator (usually the back), not in the door. You can freeze breast milk for up to three months in the freezer. You'll need to freeze it as soon as possible after expressing and certainly within a couple of hours. Remember to label the container with the date so that there is no risk of you using breast milk which has been stored for more than three months. Thaw breast milk in the refrigerator and use within 24 hours, or, if you want to use it immediately, thaw it by placing the container in a jug of warm water. Once it has reached room temperature use it at once – never refreeze it. Breast milk often separates when it's frozen, so give the bottle a good shake before offering it to your baby (*see* p.136).

Second immunisations

It's time for your baby's second set of immunisations, and it's important not to miss the appointment as he will not be thoroughly protected from the diseases until the programme is complete. Alongside the five-in-one for diptheria, whooping cough (pertussis), tetanus, Hib and polio, you will be offered a meningitis C injection. If your baby suffered any adverse affects from the first immunisations, do tell the doctor before embarking on the next set.

Expressing milk ensures that your baby continues to get all the goodness of breast milk, even when she is in someone else's care.

Sucking from a bottle is different to sucking on the breast so your baby will need to learn this new skill.

Week 13

Your baby's progress

As your baby become stronger you will notice that she spends more time practising her arm movements. Although she is able to wave her arms up and down simultaneously she hasn't yet learnt to control them, but she's working on it. Watch her practise her arm waving while she's sitting or lying on her back.

Your baby's visual skills are also increasing and she may even be able to track an object which is being moved in a circle.

Her eye contact with you is increasing, too. She's not just looking at you – this is becoming an emotional connection as she gazes at you for longer periods of time, smiles, moves her body and babbles.

Her vocabulary is enlarging and she loves the sound of her own voice – in fact you may hear her chatting away to herself in the morning when she first wakes. When you 'talk' to each other she may start to add gestures. This arm-waving shows that she's deliberately interacting with you.

Your baby was born with a keen sense of smell which continues to develop as she gets older. Already she knows your smell and that of your partner and now she's beginning to recognise other familiar scents like baby lotion and the smell of a favourite toy. Introduce her to new smells by holding items near her face and telling her what they are called. Try pleasant-smelling things such as a scented flower, a lemon or orange.

When your baby sees a colourful toy she may follow it with her eyes if you move it around, and will probably wave her arms in enjoyment.

Parents' survival guide

Mums

Grabbing a snack on the run is something most mums do, especially when the baby is small and wanting to be fed round the clock. However, eating healthily is important, as it will give you energy and make you feel better. If you are breastfeeding you should be having regular meals and drinking plenty of fluids – now is not the time to forget to eat or to think about going on a diet. If you're not breastfeeding and you want to lose weight, talk to your doctor or health visitor first. It takes a while for your body to return to normal after the birth so it may not be right for you to start a strict diet just yet.

Healthy eating doesn't have to involve hours spent in the kitchen preparing complicated meals. Many healthy foods can be eaten without the need for cooking, such as fruit and vegetables, cereals, bread, milk, yoghurt and cheese. Foods that do require cooking such as meat, poultry and fish can easily be grilled, boiled or baked.

Dads

If you are yearning for a three-course meal with all the trimmings you will probably find that you are going to have to cook it yourself, as your partner has other things on her mind. Even though life should be a bit easier now that your baby has settled into a routine of sorts, your partner is still likely to be exhausted much of the time. The really important thing for you both is to eat as much healthy food as you can so that you have the energy to keep up with your new baby's demands. Takeaways and ready-meals are all right occasionally, but certainly shouldn't make up the bulk of your diet. By supporting each other in a healthy eating plan you'll be preparing the way for when your child starts to eat the same food as you.

Milestones for week 13

Your baby...

✤ can recognise certain smells and may indicate a dislike of some of them
✤ will enjoy playing games like pat-a-cake and peek-a-boo
✤ may be able to press her feet flat on the floor when held in a standing position
✤ flaps her arms simultaneously as she tries to learn to control her movements
✤ may be beginning to show more obvious signs of emotional attachment to you.

You...

✤ understand your baby better now
✤ feel confident that you can fulfil her needs
✤ can predict more accurately when your baby will feed, sleep and be awake
✤ can make social arrangements that fit in with your baby's routines.

The big bath

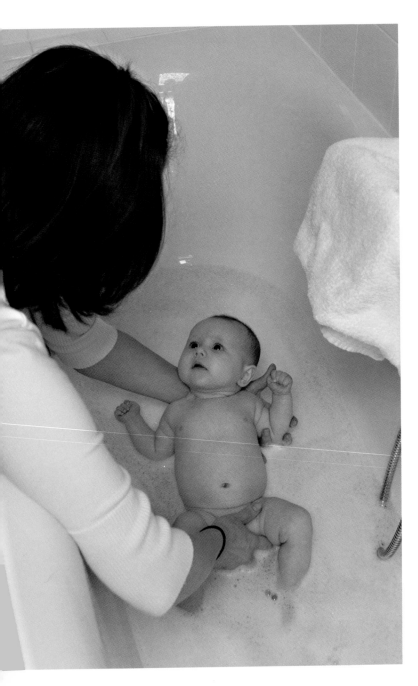

Once you have decided that your baby is ready to progress to the 'big' bath there are a few extra safety tips that you'll need to remember (see below), but otherwise the process is much the same as before (see Bathing your baby, pp.48–9). If your baby seems frightened by the big bath, or clearly isn't enjoying it, try getting in with her. She will enjoy the security of being held against you while you gently splash water over her.

Once your baby is happy about being in the big bath you could introduce some bath games such as 'swimming'. Gently move your baby up and down the bath, first on her back and then, once she's confident, on her front, holding her so that her head

Safety tips

❊ Never leave your baby or toddler alone in the bath – it takes only a few seconds for a child to drown in as little as 5 cm (2 in) of water.

❊ If you have to answer the door, wrap your baby in a towel and take her with you.

❊ When you undress your baby, don't leave her unattended on a raised surface – she could easily roll off and hurt herself.

❊ Always put the cold water in first when running the bath, then add the hot and mix well with your hand.

❊ Before putting your baby in the bath, check the temperature of the water – it should feel warm, not hot, to the skin on the inside of your wrist or elbow (a bath thermometer should read 36 °C/96 °F).

❊ Place a folded towel over the taps so that your baby won't burn herself on them.

❊ Use a non-slip bathmat in the bath.

Reassure your baby when you bathe her in a big bath, to help her overcome any intital nerves.

is supported all the time. Be very careful not to get any water on her face. If you do splash your baby's face by mistake and she's really upset, lift her out straight away and gently wipe her face dry. Suggest that she returns to the bath, but if she doesn't want to, leave bathing until another day.

Bath toys can be great fun for an older baby. Look for toys that float and bob about and containers that can be filled and emptied. Even if your baby is too young to do much more than splash about with them, she'll enjoy it if you use them to pour water over her.

Your baby may find it fun to share her bath with other children or she may prefer to bath alone. If you are intending to bath two or three children together it's best to put the youngest in first and then allow the others to join her one by one.

Hair washing

Even babies who enjoy having baths can object, often quite noisily, to having their hair washed, mainly because babies dislike having water on their faces. At first you'll find it easier to wash your baby's hair before you put her in the bath (see p.48-9). When she feels more confident about being swooshed around in the water you'll be able to shampoo her hair while she lies back and then rinse it with a jug of clean water that you set aside earlier. Make this the last thing you do before you get your baby out of the bath so that you can immediately pat her hair dry.

Once your baby can sit up unaided in the bath you can make hairwashing fun by creating weird and wacky hairstyles with the soapy hair and showing her how she looks in a mirror. If she's still reluctant, you'll have to distract her by singing or playing with a bath toy as you gently shampoo and rinse her hair.

Always have a warm towel ready to wrap your baby in as soon as you lift her from the bath.

Wrap a towel over the bath taps to ensure your baby doesn't burn herself on the hot metal.

Week 14

Your baby's progress

Your baby's grasp is becoming more refined and he'll start to open and close his fingers around an object rather than just grabbing it with his whole hand. Playing finger games such as 'This little piggy' will encourage him to work at gaining better control of them.

Your baby is probably becoming more selective about his toys; he may show a preference for a particular toy one day and then ignore it the next. He may start being selective with people, too, which can be embarrassing if someone has come specially to see him and he refuses to have anything to do with them. Don't force your baby to go to someone he obviously doesn't like; instead, encourage the visitor to communicate with him in a calm, quiet way, asking him if he wants to be picked up, and see if they can win him over.

Until now your baby has been holding and looking at things without really making the connection between touch and vision, but his brain is starting to coordinate what he can feel in his hand with what he can see. Help this process along by getting your baby to focus on the item he is holding by shaking it or making a noise with it.

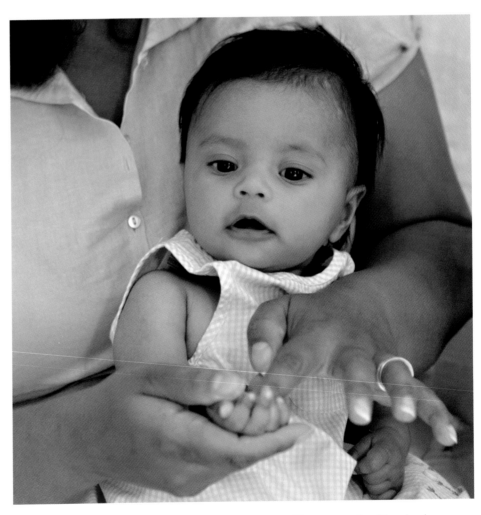

Play games such as 'Round and round the garden' with your baby. You'll notice that she takes much pleasure in using her fingers.

Parents' survival guide

Mums

It's quite normal for a relationship to be put under strain by parenthood. Perhaps you're missing your old life and the freedom and fun you used to have; you could be finding the endless round of domestic chores mind-numbingly boring and be feeling left out and lonely. This is when friendships and the support of those close to you is so important, but try as he may, it's probably unrealistic to expect your partner to fill all these gaps.

You may think that your partner is not being supportive, or doesn't understand how you are feeling. Try to remember that he's had a life-changing experience too; not only has he become a father, he may also feel that because the baby takes up so much of your time he's suddenly taken second place in your life and affections.

Unsurprisingly, all this can cause tension between you that can easily blow up into a row, but don't be surprised if the rows are about completely unrelated things, such as whose turn it is to wash up. Rows are just a way of getting all the frustrations about how you are feeling out of your system. Try to talk to each other when you are calmer and discuss how you feel. Neither of you are mind-readers, so you can't expect each other to know what's really the matter if you don't put it into words.

Dads

Communication is the key during these early weeks of parenthood. You need to understand what your partner wants so that you can help her, but she may find it hard to express her feelings. This is partly because she may not understand them herself as she struggles to adjust to her new role as a mother and homemaker.

Try to be as supportive as you can by sharing the chores and helping with the baby. Even if you work full-time make sure you are involved with the baby when you are at home, so that there doesn't come a time when she resents you for not helping. Set aside time to talk to each other, making sure that you listen to each other, too.

Milestones for week 14

Your baby...

❉ may start showing a preference for different people within the wider circle of friends and family
❉ will begin to control his fingers
❉ practises swimming movements when he's lying on his tummy
❉ will enjoy playing finger games.

You...

❉ may be feeling less tired if your baby is sleeping through the night
❉ are perhaps getting out and about more now that your baby is older and more settled
❉ may plan a night out so that you can spend some quality time with your partner.

Social behaviour

Babies' early social learning all comes from imitating the people with whom they have the most contact. A newborn soon learns to imitate some adult gestures such as poking her tongue out and yawning. This ability to imitate is one of the most important tools your baby has to help her learn about life.

Social interaction between you and your baby becomes increasingly intentional on her part during the first two months of her life, with much of her behaviour being geared towards getting you to react to her. For example, when you speak to her she will respond by making noises and wriggling her body with pleasure. This is her way of ensuring that you carry on talking to her. These early 'conversations' and the ability to imitate you are just two of the things she deliberately does to get you to respond to her.

Another way of getting your attention is crying. A baby's cries increase her mother's heart rate and, if she is breastfeeding, stimulate the production of milk. It doesn't take a young baby long to work out that her crying brings a reaction such as being offered food or picked up. By around four months your baby cries more deliberately and you'll notice her pause after crying to see if anyone will respond. This new ability to manipulate you is the beginning of some exciting discoveries for your baby.

Put your face close to your baby's when you communicate with her, so that she can watch your facial expressions and learn to imitate you as best she can.

By about six weeks your baby will have mastered the art of smiling, another social skill which she will use to her advantage. Although her first smiles are simply facial grimaces, your response to these will encourage her to go on using her facial muscles this way because she's discovered this is a guaranteed way to get you to smile back. Your baby will quickly learn to repeat things that elicit a positive response. However, if she feels the response is negative she'll be less likely to repeat an action.

By around three months your baby will start to demonstrate her enjoyment of people and will respond well to friendly, familiar faces. She'll also like activities such as having a bath or going for a walk. You'll see her showing pleasure when she recognises the routine that leads up to the activity.

Behavioural development

Your baby's behaviour is likely to change again at around seven months, when her growing awareness of herself as an individual means that she needs time and space to handle each new sight and sound. She's reached a stage in her development where she is increasingly sensitive to change, so instead of becoming more independent she goes through a phase of seeming more dependent on you than ever. She may show this by crying and clinging to you and by refusing to let you out of her sight. This attachment to you during this phase is important, as it gives her a safe base from which she can explore her new perception of herself and the world she's living in. By the time she's a year old she'll probably have grasped the idea that she exists as a separate entity, but until then she needs you to help her.

Your baby will begin to practise smiling much more frequently at 14 weeks, and will enjoy watching his own facial expressions in a mirror.

Childcare options

Good-quality childcare is in great demand, so if you are planning to go back to work at the end of your maternity leave you'll need to organise your childcare arrangements well in advance so that you can be sure that your baby gets the best care possible. If you need advice about what's available in your area, talk to your health visitor.

Family

Having your child looked after by a family member can seem the easy answer – you know the person well and can feel confident that your child will be loved and well cared for. Using a family member is also likely to be the cheapest option.

Although this might seem ideal, you'll need to be sure that your relative's ideas on bringing up children are the same as yours. If you disagree about how your child should be looked after this could lead to family rows and it's not easy to take your child's care away from a family member without causing hurt feelings. This can work the other way, too – if your mum or sister decide that they can't continue to look after your child you could be the one left feeling upset. So, if you do decide to have a family member look after your child, try to make the arrangement as business-like as possible, so that issues such as the hours, payment and expenses are discussed and agreed before you start.

Childminder

Registered childminders are regulated and graded by Ofsted. They are inspected regularly and have undergone police and health checks. Childminders are registered to care for up to three children under five (including any of their own) in their own home. Many childminders are mothers themselves, so they have had hands-on experience with babies. Their charges tend to be less than nurseries or nannies. However, you need to consider that your child will have to be taken to,

and collected from, the childminder's home, which may mean an early start to the day. Also, a childminder may not be prepared to take your baby if he is unwell, and will want time off for holidays, which may not be convenient for you.

It's important to find a childminder whose views on key issues such as feeding and discipline match yours, so you'll need to have a thorough interview with them before you agree to place your child in their care. Some childminders are

Having your mother care for your child when you go back to work allows your baby and his grandmother to get to know each other well and establish a good foundation on which to build a lasting relationship.

registered as home child carers, which means they are allowed to look after your child in your home rather than theirs.

Nanny

A nanny is another, more expensive, option and one that may only suit you if you have the room for someone to live-in, or can afford a daily nanny who lives out. Nannies don't have to be registered, so it's really important to follow up references. Look for a nanny with a recognised childcare qualification who has undergone a Criminal Record Bureau check and has a current first aid certificate. The main advantage of a nanny is that your child stays in your own home and is cared for by only one person, which gives you greater control over how he is looked after.

Au pair

An au pair is someone who has come to the UK to learn English. She (or sometimes he) will usually expect to live in your home as part of the family and to do no more than 35 hours of childcare a week. You'll have to provide a room, food and wages (although these will be a lot less than a nanny's) and give her time off to go to English lessons. Unless you're very lucky, an au pair is unlikely to have childcare qualifications apart from a liking for babies and young children, so may not be a suitable choice for full-time childcare.

Nursery care

A day nursery or a workplace crèche usually takes children from four months (sometimes younger) until they start school. Part-time places are sometimes available. State-run nurseries are often over-subscribed, so places are limited; most nurseries are privately run and prices vary. All nurseries are Ofsted registered and are inspected regularly to ensure they reach the required standard. The staff are usually a mixture of qualified and unqualified carers who look after a small number of children at any one time. Nurseries are open at least 50 weeks of the year, so they provide a reliable source of care. It's well worth visiting a number of nurseries before making a decision, looking for a warm, welcoming atmosphere, cheerful staff, happy children and a good recent Ofsted report.

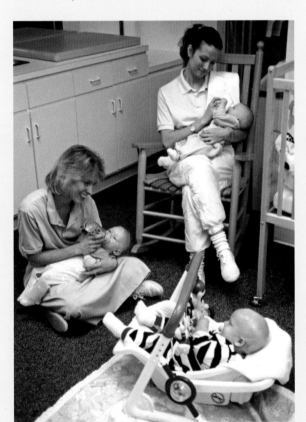

For many babies, their first experience of socialising with other babies is at day nursery.

Week 15

Your baby's progress

Your baby's legs are becoming stronger all the time, and when you hold him upright on a flat surface he may try to balance on his feet for a few seconds. You can help him strengthen his legs by giving him plenty of exercise; hold him round the waist and encourage him to jump up and down on your lap. He may enjoy spending short periods – no more than 10 to 15 minutes – in a baby bouncer.

Dads tend to play with their babies differently to mums. Your partner is probably more physical with your baby, flying him through the air and bouncing him up and down on his knee. He'll love this and will probably laugh out loud, unless the play is so vigorous that he becomes frightened. Then there will be tears and he'll probably turn to you for comfort.

Bath time can be great fun, too, as any fears of the water he may have had when he was younger are likely to have gone. Water play is a great way to stimulate your baby's senses and he'll enjoy playing with toys in the bath and finding out all the fun things he can do with water. Try splashing him gently (taking care not to get water in his face) and see just how quickly he learns to splash himself.

Your baby may have a good attention span and be able to concentrate on something for a while, or he may lose interest very quickly. You can help increase your baby's attention span by giving him plenty of one-to-one attention, perhaps by reading to him or playing a game in which he can participate such as 'peek-a-boo'.

Now that he can prop himself up on his front, your baby can see things from a different angle.

Parents' survival guide

Mums

You may want to think about parental leave now – for yourself if you plan to return to your old job, and also for your partner if he's in full-time employment. Parental leave is a period of unpaid time off work that the government allows new parents to help them strike a better balance between work and family commitments. If you and your partner have worked for your employers for over a year you'll probably find that you are each entitled to take 13 weeks of unpaid leave for every child that you have. This has to be taken before the child's fifth birthday, or within five years of adopting. If you are claiming disability living for your child you'll be allowed 18 weeks, which has to be taken before your child is 18 years of age. Parental leave can be taken in short or long blocks, depending on what is agreed with your employer, but generally these blocks are in multiples of one week with a maximum of four weeks in any one year.

Dads

Unpaid leave may not be something you feel you can consider right now, especially if you are struggling to make ends meet because you have more expense or there is less money coming in than before. But it's certainly worth finding out about, even if you don't use it until your child is older. Along with parental leave you are also entitled to take unpaid time off work for a family emergency, and that includes occurrences such as organising appropriate childcare in special circumstances, for example if your partner has to go into hospital.

Milestones for week 15

Your baby...

❉ probably enjoys more vigorous play, such as 'flying' and bouncing up and down

❉ can have a lot of fun in the bath playing with toys, bubbles and sponges

❉ may be able to track objects that are less than 2.5 cm (1 in) wide with his eyes

❉ may be lifting his shoulders higher off the ground when he is lying on his tummy.

You...

❉ should check whether your baby needs a bigger car seat now

❉ may find that your baby begins to settle on his own when you put him down for the night

❉ may want to consider getting a baby bouncer. If you decide to buy second-hand, check that there are no broken parts and that instructions for use are included.

Out and about with your baby

There's no 'right time' to start taking your baby out, so unless you've been told otherwise for health reasons, you can both start going out as soon as you feel ready. At first it's best to avoid very crowded places where you will be jostled and your baby may be exposed to people's coughs and colds, but other than that, provided you take a few sensible precautions, your baby should be able to go anywhere you go.

When you are dressing your baby you'll need to remember that she can't regulate her body temperature as well as you are able to, so to start with it's best to put on one more layer than you would wear in the same environment. This will stop your baby getting cold. Make sure that the extra layer of clothing is something that can easily be removed if you find that she's too warm. This is important when you go from the outside into a warm environment such as a supermarket or shopping centre, where your baby could quickly become overheated if she is wrapped up too much.

A hat is one item of clothing your baby should always wear when she's out. Much heat is lost through the head, so a warm hat will help to prevent your baby from losing too much heat in the winter. In summer a sunhat will protect her from sunburn.

Babies are particularly vulnerable to the effects of the sun because their skin is thinner and, therefore, more susceptible to sunburn than an adult's. This is why young babies under six months should always be kept out of the sun, and older babies should be protected by covering them up and by using a high-protection sunscreen on any exposed skin.

Changing bag

You don't have to buy a special changing bag, though they can be convenient as they usually have a waterproof lining and an integral changing mat, as well as lot of useful pockets. However, any big bag will do, just so long as it will hold everything you will need when you are out and about with your baby. The essentials are:

- a changing mat or small towel
- spare nappies
- nappy bags (for soiled nappies)
- baby wipes
- a small pot of barrier cream
- a change of baby clothes
- sterilised bottle, teat and cap, cooled boiled water and infant formula (if bottle-feeding)
- muslin cloths to mop up any sick and dribble
- sunscreen
- a favourite toy.

A well-stocked changing bag will support all your baby's needs, allowing you both to make the most of your days out together.

On sunny days, always cover your baby in sunscreen, even if she is going to be mostly in the shade, as babies are particularly susceptible to sunburn.

Transporting your baby

Whatever type of travel system you have, you need to be able to lie your baby down flat for the first three months. It's not until six months, once she's gained control of her head, that she can sit upright in a pram, buggy or stroller.

Safety for prams and pushchairs

❋ Make sure the pram/pushchair is suitable for a newborn.

❋ Always use a safety harness. Check your pram or pushchair has an integral five-point harness and the carrycot has D-rings to enable you to attach a harness.

❋ Always put the brakes on, even on a flat surface.

❋ Remove the rain covers when you are indoors to prevent your baby from becoming overheated.

❋ Don't carry an older child on your baby's pram or pushchair unless it's designed for two children.

❋ Always check that the safety lock which prevents the chassis from collapsing is working.

❋ Don't hang shopping bags from the handles.

Baby carriers

If you are out and about on foot you may find it easier to carry a young baby in a sling or carrier. These offer ideal ways of keeping your baby held snugly against you while leaving your hands free. Many baby carriers adapt from front-facing for a newborn to outward-facing, which is suitable for babies once they are three months old. From about six months your baby will enjoy sitting in a carrier on your back, which affords her a different view, so you may want to invest in a framed back carrier at this stage. Always try the carrier on before you buy

Most car seats for small babies can be removed from the car and carried by a handle.

Safety for baby carriers

✿ Make sure the straps are adjusted correctly so that both you and your baby are comfortable.

✿ Ensure that your newborn's head is well supported.

✿ Check the buckles and straps regularly for wear and tear.

✿ Use a harness to secure your baby safely in a back carrier.

it to make sure that it is comfortable and that you can get it off and on without help. It's also a good idea to check that the carrier is washable.

Car seats

If you have a car your baby must always travel in a car seat, which should be placed in the back if you have a front-seat airbag. For safety, your baby's first car seat should be backward-facing to give him added protection if you are involved in an accident. It's important to ensure the seat is installed correctly – many stores offer a fitting service. Not all car seats fit all cars, so check the seat you buy is suitable for your vehicle. It'll make life easier for you if the seat covers are removable and washable.

Safety in cars

✿ Make sure that the five-point harness adjusts easily.

✿ The car seat back should support your baby's head.

✿ Check the seat is suitable for your child's weight, which is more important than age.

✿ The seat you buy should comply with safety standard ECE R44/03.

✿ Never buy second-hand. The seat could have been damaged in an accident.

Buying second-hand

Although buying second-hand baby equipment can save you money, never buy items that could have been damaged, such as a car seat. Before you purchase an item make sure that the operating instructions are with it as these are essential for safe installation and use. You also need to check that the item meets current safety requirements. For more information or a free leaflet on buying second-hand baby equipment, contact the Baby Products Association (BPA) helpline: 0845 4569570.

Your baby may fall asleep in the car but you should never leave him unattended. Always take him with you.

Week 16

Your baby's progress

Your four-month-old baby will probably have nearly doubled his birth weight. Much of this additional weight is fat, which not only provides your baby with insulation but also stores nutrients. Some babies have a growth spurt about now and your baby may seem extra-hungry. Although giving solids such as baby rice is not generally recommended before six months, if your baby seems unsatisfied at the end of each feed ask your health visitor for advice. Babies are individuals and some need solids earlier than others.

Whether your baby seems hungrier than usual or not, he'll probably be feeding less often now. His stomach has grown so that he can manage more milk at each feed, which means he doesn't need to eat so frequently.

Your baby is reaching a stage when everything he manages to get hold of goes straight into his mouth. This 'mouthing' of objects is another way of exploring the world around him and helps him discover different tastes and textures.

You may find that your baby seems to be taking more notice of things going on around him. Watch for moments when he becomes quiet as you talk to him and then 'talks' back once you've finished. When he does this he's learning about listening and waiting for a response, which is the foundation for conversation.

At around this age your baby is now beginning to understand that a toy still exists, even when it has disappeared from view. Although he may make no attempt to look for a favourite object that he has dropped, he'll show signs of delight when you pick it up and give it back to him.

Your baby will quickly learn to amuse himself if you give him stimulating toys to play with when he is alone in his cot.

Parents' survival guide

Mums

Don't leave getting your baby a passport to the very last minute before you need it. If there's a chance you could be taking him abroad in the next few months, get a passport application form from the Post Office, Passport Office or a branch of WorldChoice travel agents, or ring the UK Passport Services' Application Form Request line on 0901 4700110. Alternatively, you can fill in a form online on the UK Passport Services' website (www.ukpa.gov.uk) and print it out. You'll need to send in the form with two identical photographs, one of them validated to say that it is a true likeness of your baby, and his full birth certificate (*see* p.41). If you don't have this you'll need to get one from the registrar in the area where he was born. Also required is a document that proves that your child is British. This can be your own or your partner's birth certificate, or a Home Office certificate of registration or naturalisation, or your UK passport (if it was valid at the time of your baby's birth).

It's a good idea to use the Check & Send service which is available at Worldchoice travel agents and selected post offices. Although there is a charge for this, it does mean that your application won't be returned because you have filled in the form incorrectly, or have forgotten to enclose a key document. Using this service speeds up the process, too, and could save you as much as a week in waiting time.

Dads

Your baby's going to need photos for his passport, so you may want to get your camera ready. Alternatively, you can use a photo booth, but it's usually easier to take the picture yourself, or to get someone your baby is familiar with to take it. However, the specifications are now very strict, so check them online at www.ukpa.gov.uk or phone the Adviceline on 0870 521 0410. The key things you'll need to take into consideration are that your baby needs to be against an off-white, cream or light grey plain background so that his features can be clearly seen. He must be on his own, with no toys or dummies, and he must be facing the camera so that his full face is in view.

Milestones for week 16

Your baby...

❋ may have his third series of immunisations around now
❋ probably tries to put everything he can get hold of into his mouth
❋ can reach out and will try to grab objects held in front of him
❋ may enjoy playing quietly with his hands and feet
❋ will start to pay more attention to things that are going on around him
❋ may show signs of listening and responding when you 'talk' to each other.

You...

❋ may want to consider planning a holiday and will need to organise your baby's passport if you're going abroad
❋ may be concerned about knowing what to do if your baby becomes ill
❋ may want to consider taking a first aid course.

Going away with your baby

Whether you are going away for a weekend break in this country or planning a trip overseas, organisation is the key when it comes to taking your baby on holiday. Once you've decided where you are going, write a list of everything you think you may need while you are away. It'll look frightening at first – in fact you may start wondering if it's really worth the effort – but once you've cut out all the non-essentials you'll find that the list has become much more manageable.

The right travel equipment will help smooth your journey and allow you to explore once you've arrived. If your baby is under three months old, having your travel system with you will take some of the hassle out of getting in and out of cars and planes. If your baby is older you may want to put him in a lightweight buggy which you can usually take up to the aircraft steps. After that, until you are reunited with the buggy, you'll have to carry your baby as well as everything else you have with

you. Putting everything into a shoulder bag or rucksack will leave your hands free. Alternatively, you could put your baby in a sling and carry your bags.

Check your travel arrangements several weeks before you are due to depart and make sure that you have travel insurance and your new European Health Insurance card (this has replaced

Take away checklist

Your baby will need:
- ❉ a car seat, unless you've arranged to hire one with the car (it must be the correct size for your child's age and weight)
- ❉ a pram, buggy or similar
- ❉ a travel cot (unless your accommodation has a cot)
- ❉ baby clothes
- ❉ a baby blanket and muslin cloths, or washable bibs
- ❉ a nappy bag (with enough nappies for the first few days, wipes, travel changing mat, nappy sacks and barrier cream)
- ❉ breast pump and bottles if you're breastfeeding
- ❉ formula, bottles and feeding equipment if you're bottle feeding
- ❉ sterilising tablets and a container (for cold-water sterilising)
- ❉ a first aid kit (thermometer, baby paracetamol, antiseptic ointment, plasters, tweezers, insect repellent, calamine lotion, rehydration powder)
- ❉ sunscreen and a sun hat
- ❉ a few favourite toys.

Putting on a CD of favourite nursery rhymes on a long journey will help to keep your baby entertained while travelling.

the old E111). You'll find more information about this on the Department of Health website at www.dh.gov.uk/traveller. Tell your airline that you are travelling with a baby – some have sky cots on long-haul flights (you'll need to book these in advance), while others will allocate you special seats.

If you are flying it's a good idea to get your baby to suck, either from the breast or a bottle, on take off and landing as this will stop his ears hurting. If you find you've forgotten something, ask the cabin crew if they can help. Many airlines have a small supply of useful items such as nappies on board.

If you're travelling by car, allow plenty of time as you will have to stop often to feed and change your baby. Be prepared to keep him amused by singing songs and chatting to him about things you see outside the car. Take a rug or blanket with you so that when you stop your baby has somewhere to lie where he can kick and play for a while after his feed. If it's hot, you may want to fit removable blinds on the car window to keep your baby well-shaded while you're travelling. Never leave your sleeping baby in the car once you've arrived at your destination; he could become overheated in just a few minutes.

Safety in the sun

Always keep your baby out of direct sunlight, especially during the middle of the day when the sun is at its strongest, as his skin will burn very easily. You'll need to protect any bare skin with a sun protection cream made for babies. When you are outdoors, make sure that he wears a sunhat and have a parasol attached to the buggy to give him additional shelter from the sun. Babies can become overheated very quickly, so keep your baby cool by dressing him in loose, light cotton clothes. You can find more sun safety tips on www.sunsmart.org.uk.

Always cover your baby's head with a sunhat if he is to be in the sun for any length of time.

Childhood diseases

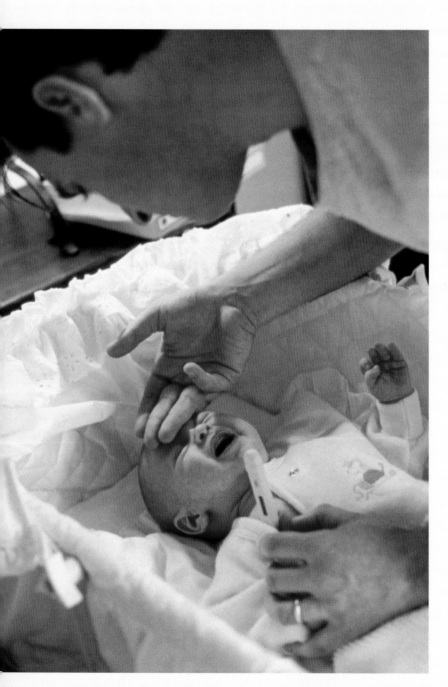

Once your child has been immunised against diseases such as measles and whooping cough he is unlikely to be affected by them – in fact many childhood diseases have all but disappeared in this country because the immunisation programme has been so successful. Being immunised doesn't always prevent a child from catching a disease, but it does mean that it will be in a very mild form which is unlikely to cause any complications. The important thing is for you to be able to recognise the symptoms of a disease at an early stage so that you can take the appropriate action.

Immunisation reminder

It's time for your baby's third set of immunisations. Even though he's already had two sets of injections, don't miss the appointment – your baby will not be as well protected from the diseases until the programme is complete. Alongside the five-in-one for diptheria, whooping cough (pertussis), tetanus, Hib and polio your child will be offered a meningitis C and pneumococcus injection at four months. The meningitis C and pneumococcal immunisations are repeated again at twelve months. This is followed by the MMR (measles, mumps and rubella) and pneumococcus at 13 months. If you're in a high-risk area, or there is a family history of TB (tuberculosis), your baby may also be offered immunisation against TB with a BCG vaccine. If your baby suffered adverse effects from any of the previous injections make sure you tell the doctor.

Although taking your baby's temperature can be helpful, don't rely on the thermometer reading alone. Often, babies can be ill when their temperature is at normal or below normal.

Chickenpox and whooping cough

Chickenpox

Although it is highly infectious, chickenpox is usually a mild disease if it's caught during childhood and it rarely occurs in babies under one year old. It's caused by one of the herpes group of viruses and is transmitted by direct contact with an infected person. The incubation period of this disease is 14 to 21 days and your child will be most infectious before the rash appears, which makes it hard to isolate an infected child from others.

Symptoms Chickenpox results in a fever and headache followed by a rash, although sometimes the only symptom is the rash. At first the rash, which appears as small red spots which quickly turn into itchy blisters, can be seen mainly on the trunk and then spreads to the rest of the body. The blisters dry to form crusts which remain in place for a few weeks. Scars occur when the spots are scratched or become infected. Your child will remain infectious until new blisters have stopped appearing, which can take up to a week or more.

Treatment Reduce the fever (*see* p.60) and keep your child's nails short to prevent him from scratching and infecting the spots. Calamine lotion can be soothing, and having a bath with a handful of bicarbonate of soda added to it will ease the itchiness. Dress your child in loose clothing and give him plenty of drinks. You should consult your doctor if the spots become infected.

Whooping cough (pertussis)

This can be very serious in the case of babies under one year of age. The incubation period is seven to ten days and the disease is spread through droplet infection. Your child will be infectious from around two days before the onset of the cough until about 21 days later, although the cough itself can last for up to as long as ten weeks.

Symptoms Whooping cough starts with a slight cough and sneezing and then develops into severe bouts of up to 20 short, dry coughs which occur during the day and night, but are often worse at night. In children over 18 months of age a long attack of coughing may be followed by a sharp intake of breath which produces the whooping sound.

Treatment Stay with your child during his coughing fits because they can be very distressing. Keep a bowl handy in case your child vomits and clean up any sickness immediately, using disinfectant to help prevent the infection spreading. If possible, try to distract your child from coughing.

Applying calamine lotion will help to relieve the itching of chickenpox spots.

Measles, mumps and rubella

Fortunately measles, mumps and rubella (German measles) are unlikely to affect your child if he's under six months because he'll still be protected by your immunity, provided you have been vaccinated yourself. At around 13 months your child will be offered the MMR vaccine to protect him from these diseases.

Measles

This is a very infectious viral disease which is spread through droplets from the nose and throat of an infected person. The incubation period is seven to twelve days and your child becomes infectious about six days before the rash appears and for five days afterwards.

Symptoms The first symptoms are a raised temperature, runny nose, cough, redness of the eyes, lethargy and loss of appetite. A couple of days later tiny white spots appear on the inside of the cheeks. These are followed by a red rash which starts behind the ears and on the face and then spreads to the chest and the rest of the body. The rash is not itchy but it will be accompanied by a high fever. As the rash fades your child's temperature should fall.

Treatment Reduce the fever (*see* p.60) and if your child's eyes have become encrusted wipe them with cotton wool dipped in cooled boiled water. You will need to call the doctor if your child is no better three days after the rash appears, if his fever is very high or if he develops other symptoms such as earache or breathing difficulties.

Mumps

Caused by a virus, mumps is spread by droplets. The incubation period is 12 to 21 days and your child will be infectious for two days before the swelling appears.

Symptoms Pain and swelling in the glands in one or both sides of the face, neck and jaw. These symptoms may be accompanied by fever and a headache. The swelling makes the face appear puffy and reaches its maximum in about two days, subsiding within five days.

Treatment Give suitable pain relief and apply warmth to the swollen areas. Your child should be given easy-to-swallow foods such as jelly and ice cream and plenty of liquids. Call your doctor if your child develops pains in the stomach, or, if a boy, has a red testicle.

Rubella (German measles)

Rubella is caused by a virus and is spread through coughing and sneezing by an infected person. The incubation period is 10 to 21 days and your child will be infectious from the day before the rash appears and for two days after this. Although usually a mild disease in children (in fact it can go unnoticed), it's very important to keep your child away from pregnant women as rubella can cause serious harm to an unborn baby in the first half of a pregnancy.

Symptoms The first sign is usually a rash made up of tiny pink spots which are not blotchy or raised above the skin's surface. These appear on the face and then spread to the trunk. The rash is not itchy and only lasts for two to three days. It may be accompanied by a runny nose, redness round the eyes and swollen glands at the back of the neck.

Treatment Keep a check on your child's temperature, apply fever-reducing measures if necessary (*see* p.60) and give plenty of fluids. Call your doctor for confirmation of rubella if you are unsure, but don't take your child to the surgery because of the risk to pregnant women.

Meningitis and septicaemia

Meningitis is the inflammation of the lining of the brain and spinal cord. There are two kinds of meningitis: bacterial, which can be life-threatening, and viral, which is usually less serious. The bacterial form of meningitis carries the risk of bacteria entering the blood stream which can lead to meningococcal septicaemia (blood poisoning). Septicaemia is a very dangerous form of bacterial infection and needs emergency treatment. Viral meningitis usually requires no specific treatment.

Symptoms The early signs of meningitis and septicaemia are similar to the symptoms of other childhood diseases, but the baby will usually get ill more quickly and get worse faster. This is why both parents and healthcare professionals need to be watchful if a child has a feverish illness, especially when the cause is not apparent. Be aware of the signs to look out for that could indicate meningitis and septicaemia (*see* right).

Treatment If your baby seems very sick and shows some of the signs which could indicate meningitis without a rash, don't wait for the rash to appear. Contact your doctor immediately or go to the nearest A & E department where your baby will be given antibiotics as a safety precaution, before other diagnostic tests are done. The early treatment of bacterial meningitis and septicaemia with antibiotics will give the baby the best chance of making a full recovery. However, if viral meningitis is then diagnosed the antibiotics given will make no difference to the outcome of the disease. Usually it's a question of waiting for the body's natural defences to overcome it.

For more information on this illness, contact the Meningitis Trust on www.meningitis-trust.org, or their 24-hour telepone helpline on 0800 028 18 28; or the Meningitis Research Foundation on www.meningitis.org, 24-hour telephone helpline: 080 8800 3344.

What to look out for

Your baby may show some or all of the following signs:

* a high-pitched moaning cry
* refusal to feed
* fever
* vomiting
* cold hands and feet
* very sleepy and hard to wake
* pale or blotchy skin
* tense or bulging fontanelle (soft spot)
* being irritable when picked up
* a stiff body with jerky movements or else floppy and lifeless
* red or purple spots that do not fade when you press a glass over them are a sign of septicaemia. These are harder to spot on black skin, so check the soles of the feet and palms of the hands.

Immunisation

HiB and meningococcal C immunisations, which are now part of the immunisation programme, protect against two specific bacterial causes of meningitis and pneumonia. There is no immunisation against viral meningitis.

If you notice red or purple spots on your baby, press a glass over them to test for meningitis – if the rash doesn't fade, call 999.

Week 17

Your baby's progress

You may notice that your baby is beginning to rotate her wrist when she holds a toy so that she can see it from different angles. Encourage this wrist movement by teaching her how to wave goodbye. Do the movement yourself, then raise her arm and gently move it up and down. She'll soon master this move and will delight in waving at people.

Your baby will play with her fingers a lot now as she begins to understand how they work. This finger play will help her develop the fine motor skills she will need as she gets older. You can help her along by propping her up safely into a sitting position so that she can watch her hands as she manipulates them to see what they can do.

Around this time you may find that your baby starts to show a fondness for a particular toy or comforter. This is a big step in her emotional development, as it is her first attachment other than to her parents and carers. You can encourage this step towards independence by making sure that the toy or comforter is always there for her when she needs it.

Your baby is probably showing her emotions in other ways, too. She may express herself more through play now, banging her toys when she becomes excited, frustrated or angry. She may also have learnt to comfort herself by sucking her fingers or her thumb. Don't discourage this, as it's her way of coping with emotional upsets.

At 17 weeks your baby may have formed an attachment to an object, such as a favourite toy or blanket, and will enjoy 'mouthing' it to comfort himself.

Parents' survival guide

Mums

During pregnancy the bond between a mother and daughter usually becomes stronger, so that when the baby arrives your mother will probably be second on the scene after your partner. The shared experience of childbirth is likely to draw you and your mother even closer together, and you'll probably be turning to her for a lot of support right now. If your partner's finding it hard to understand your sudden need to have your mother around all the time, try to explain your feelings to him.

Your parents and your partner's parents now have a new role in life as grandparents which, if handled correctly, can have many benefits for you all, and especially for your child. Traditionally, grandparents are considered to spoil their grandchildren, but this isn't necessarily a bad thing, provided it doesn't interfere with the way you want your child brought up. It may be wise to set down some guidelines about how you see their roles so that there are no misunderstandings. Talk to your partner first, so that you are both in agreement about how much involvement you want the grandparents to have.

Dads

Now that you have a baby you'll probably be seeing more of your partner's parents than you ever have before. Try not to see their enthusiasm as interference – it's natural that they want to be involved in your child's life. As well as being willing and trusted babysitters, they can share the experience and knowledge of another generation with your child when she's older. To be loved and nurtured by grandparents is something very special and a great gift to be able to give your child.

Milestones for week 17

Your baby...

* is learning to identify and locate different sounds
* may be able to calm herself when she becomes upset
* shows signs of attachment towards a particular toys or comforter
* will enjoy playing with her fingers
* might be able to wave and enjoy the reaction she gets from others when she does.

You...

* may find that your baby becomes clingy when you try leaving her with others
* may want to consider leaving her with grandparents while you have a couple of days away
* may start considering going back to work part-time or job-sharing with a colleague who is in a similar position as you.

Learning separation

Some babies want to be held and soothed all of the time, so that if you put them down they cry inconsolably until they are picked up again. This can be pretty frustrating, as it leaves you with little time to get on with other things. Try to be patient – your baby isn't deliberately being difficult, she just needs the reassurance of knowing you are there. She has to learn to feel comfortable and secure in the world around her. By responding to her need to be close to you, you will be helping her gain in confidence so that she will eventually be happy to spend brief periods physically separated from you without anxiety.

You'll find that as your baby grows in confidence and trust she'll start to spend time away from you without fuss. This is a gradual process, and not one that you can hurry. Lying awake and quiet in her cot means that she's feeling secure about being alone, but this may take time to achieve.

From around twelve weeks your baby will become more aware of her environment, so you could try hanging mobiles over her cot, or giving her other safe cot toys to see if they'll amuse her when she first opens her eyes in the morning. Of course if she wakes hungry no amount of toys will pacify her, but if this is not the case you may find that she plays quietly by herself for a little while. Once she can do this she's taken her first small step towards independence.

In the meantime you could try carrying your baby in a sling while you get on with the things you need to do such as housework or shopping. Being held against you in this way should give her all the reassurance she needs. Getting your partner to take her for a while, or giving her to a friend or grandparent to hold while you stay close by, may also be a way of relieving the situation. But sometimes only you will do, and until she's outgrown this phase the best thing you can do is cuddle her.

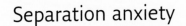

Separation anxiety

At about six months your baby begins to understand that you and she are two separate people. This can seem very scary for her, so her way of dealing with this is to cling to you more than usual. Be prepared for her to literally hang on to you throughout the day and to have difficulty going to sleep at night. Even if she's been sleeping through the night for some time before this, she may start to wake and call out for you. This is her way of trying to restore the feeling of togetherness she's been used to. This syndrome, known as separation anxiety, occurs between six to eight months and usually passes within a couple of months. However, separation anxiety often occurs again at around two years of age when your baby is having to cope with her growing sense of independence.

If your baby needs to be held a lot, carry her in a sling so your hands will be free to get on with your chores.

Reassuring your baby by keeping him close when he needs you to will give him a sense of security.

Week 18

Your baby's progress

Your baby's grasp is improving all the time and you may notice that instead of just holding a toy by curling his fingers around it, he is now beginning to use his thumb to grasp with as well. This new achievement will increase his ability to handle and manipulate objects. Your baby needs this skill as his hand-eye coordination develops and he begins to understand how big an object is, how far away it is and how to reach out and grasp it.

Your baby's attention span is increasing, and he may spend more time playing with his toys now. He may prefer toys that move, make noises or have an interesting texture. He will have the most fun if you play with him too, so talk to him about the toys he seems interested in and encourage him to explore their potential.

Conversations with your baby have probably developed a pattern, with each of you taking turns to 'talk'. Your baby is starting to anticipate when you are going to speak – you can see this in his body movements and in the way he watches your facial expressions as you talk to him. Hold your baby facing you and watch as he tries to copy your facial expressions. Try exaggerating them – stick out your tongue or open your mouth really wide, for example – and see how he reacts to this. These early conversations are laying the foundations for your baby's speech development later on.

Your baby will probably be discovering the opposable use of his thumbs now – a valuable addition to his growing set of skills.

Parents' survival guide

Mums

You've probably been going to your local parent and baby group, where you'll have made friends with other parents with babies around the same age as yours. You may all now be thinking about other areas of activity you can get your babies involved in. There can be fierce competition between mums determined that their babies will be high achievers when it comes to outside activities, so you may be happier standing back until yours is older.

There are plenty of 'baby clubs' available covering activities ranging from yoga, gym and swimming through to music. All of them claim to offer babies and, in some cases, toddlers advantages that they wouldn't otherwise have. Although some of these claims may be true, it's worth remembering that none of these clubs are crucial to your baby's development, so don't feel under pressure to join unless you really want to.

If you prefer staying at home with your baby, visiting friends or having local mums in for coffee, that's fine too. The important thing is that you don't feel lonely and isolated, and that your baby has other children to play with who may eventually become his friends.

Dads

Many baby clubs operate during the day only, so it can be hard for you to join them. You could try asking your local leisure centre if they run classes that are suitable for you and your baby; you may find that there are parent and baby swimming classes at weekends. Some gyms offer their members crèche facilities, and although this is not the same as a baby club it can be a good way of getting out yourself while your baby spends time in the company of others. At first you'll need to stay with him until he gets used to the idea. The crèche should be registered with the local health authority and staffed by qualified carers who look after a limited number of children at any one time.

Milestones for week 18

Your baby...

- is becoming stronger every day and may now be able to lift his head, neck and shoulders off the floor
- is beginning to learn about cause and effect and will soon begin to understand about object permanence
- probably shows a growing interest in people and may respond negatively to strangers if they frighten him
- may be able to recognise himself when he looks in the mirror.

You...

- should check that you have a well-stocked first aid kit
- are perhaps feeling less tired if your baby has started to sleep through the night
- could join the local library so that you can borrow lots of different books to look at with your baby.

New reasons for crying

As your baby grows older and better at communicating his needs, his reasons for crying will start to change. Of course he will still cry if he's tired or hungry, but you are likely to be settled into a routine now so you'll be able to anticipate his needs before he becomes too upset.

Anxiety could become a new reason for crying, although this may not happen until he's around six months of age. Your baby may cry when you leave him, or just move out of his sight. This is because he's only just beginning to realise that you and he are separate entities and he's still unsure of how to cope without you. Be sure to tell him that you are leaving, even if it's only to go to another room for a minute. He may cry, but as long as you always return, he'll learn not to be anxious that you'll disappear without warning.

Changes to his routine can also make him anxious. Perhaps you've returned to work and have had to leave him with a childminder, or maybe you also have an older child that you now have to get off to school in the morning. If possible, try to start any new routine gradually so that your baby has some time to become accustomed to the changes.

Your baby is becoming more aware of his surroundings; he may be particularly sensitive to sound, in which case he will easily be frightened by a loud noise, either domestic or from the street outside. Even raised or angry voices can upset a baby and make him cry. Give your baby plenty of cuddles and reassurance if he's frightened. As long as he knows that you are there with him he'll soon be comforted and reassured.

An older baby spends a lot of time trying to do things that are beyond his capabilities, which in turn leads to frustration and crying. You can't avoid this, but you can make it easier for him by helping him to achieve his aim. Perhaps he's trying to grasp something and you can help by putting the object

Baby's pain barrier

Pain is another reason for tears. As your baby becomes more mobile he has more chance of hurting himself and, no matter how careful you are, he's going to bump into things. Usually it's shock that makes him cry rather than any actual injury. Plenty of cuddles and perhaps a gentle rub or kiss to the affected area will help to stop any tears. Discomfort caused by teething can also cause tears as cutting teeth can be a really painful business (*see* p.126 for more information on teething).

within his reach, or maybe he's trying to crawl and putting your hands behind his feet will help him move forward.

Some babies are frightened by new experiences which they can't associate with their everyday lives. For example, if you live in a town a trip to the country may produce some scary animals such as sheep and cows. Even simple things like a plane going overhead can cause distress if it's unfamiliar. Give your baby lots of cuddles and reassurance, and he'll soon realise these things won't hurt him.

Now that he is older your baby is more likely to cry because he is fearful or anxious.

You will be more able to anticipate your baby's everyday needs now so she is less likely to be upset because of hunger or tiredness.

Week 19

Your baby's progress

Every week your baby's mobility increases and, by now, she may be rolling over from her back to her front. At first this may happen accidentally as she manoeuvres herself towards a toy which is slightly out of reach. But once she's worked out how she's managed it, she'll do it deliberately. Never leave your child unattended on a raised surface. This is especially important once she can roll herself over as she may topple onto the floor and hurt herself.

As your baby's depth of vision increases you may notice her actively looking around the room to identify something that is making a noise she can hear, or see her eyes follow a moving object when you are outside. This is known as visual scanning, which is a skill she will need when she begins to read. Spend time with your baby looking at books and pictures in magazines and talk to her about what she can see.

You may notice that your baby reacts to your moods. If you're happy, smiling and laughing she may be too, but if you are in a bad mood or are feeling upset you may find that she responds in the same way by being cross or by crying for no apparent reason. Although your baby is too young to really understand your moods she may be distressed by angry voices or sullen silences, so try to keep your mood upbeat when you're with her, even if you don't feel like it.

If your baby becomes upset the best way to comfort her is by holding and perhaps gently rocking her. Some babies find listening to white noise soothing so turning on the vacuum cleaner or running the washing machine or dishwasher could settle your baby. Alternatively a car ride has been known to work wonders.

Your baby's increased strength and confidence allows her to begin rolling from her back onto her front deliberately.

With every roll, your baby is developing her control and preparing herself for learning to crawl later on.

Parents' survival guide

Mums

If you haven't got round to making an appointment with your dentist, now might be a good time to do so. It's important to have a dental check-up to make sure that your teeth and gums are healthy. NHS dental treatment is free for twelve months after the birth, so you'll want to get any treatment done during this period. When you claim for dental treatment you must show the Exemption Certificate you were given during pregnancy, or your dentist may give you a form to fill in.

It's also worth remembering that not only does your baby qualify for free prescriptions until she's 16 years old, but you are also entitled to free prescriptions for twelve months from the birth. If you didn't have any prescriptions during your pregnancy but need one now, ask your doctor or Jobcentre Plus for leaflet P11 NHS Prescriptions and fill in form A.

Dads

If you have concerns about what you are entitled to now that you are a family, or have questions about your employment rights or housing issues, you could talk to someone at your local Citizens Advice Bureau (CAB). You will find their address in your local phone book or you can use their online service at www.adviceguide.org.uk. The CAB offers free information and advice on a wide range of topics, including benefits, housing, employment, debt and consumer and legal issues.

Milestones for week 19

Your baby...

* is likely to be becoming more mobile and may be able to roll right over
* can scan a room and follow a moving object with her eyes as her vision improves
* may be able to transfer an object from one hand to the other
* can probably soothe herself when she becomes upset, although she still needs comfort from you.

You...

* may need to consider buying safety items such as stair gates and socket covers for when your baby becomes mobile
* should try to avoid rows and upsets when you're with your baby.

Books for babies

It's never too early to introduce your baby to books; from as early as twelve weeks she will enjoy sitting with you looking at simple coloured images. First books need to have easy-to-understand bright pictures and should be made from materials that will withstand some rough treatment. Board books, soft cloth books and waterproof bath books are good choices as they will all stand up to enthusiastic handling from your baby.

There are so many first books to choose from you are bound to find one that will quickly become a favourite. Look for books with different textures on each page that will teach your baby about touch, or lift-the-flap books and those that make noises to introduce an element of excitement. She will like looking at books with pictures of familiar things such as a dog, a car or a ball. Begin by turning the pages slowly and naming the pictures. You are tuning your baby into the concept of two-dimensional

representations of real life objects, and also that books read from front to back and from left to right. She will enjoy the ritual of looking at the page, listening to you talking about what she can see, then helping to turn the page. As the book becomes familiar she will start to anticipate what will come next when each page is turned.

Books can become part of your baby's bedtime routine, allowing you to spend a calm, happy time together before sleep. But don't just reserve them for bedtime; make time for a quiet session during the day as well.

Although your child is too young to understand the significance of these first books, this early familiarity with them will hopefully start an enjoyment of books and reading which will continue throughout her life.

Bookstart

This is a national programme which aims to promote a life-long love of reading by giving free books to babies, toddlers and pre-school children. It's usually coordinated through the library service, but sometimes through local education or health services. The first pack, which is for babies from nought to twelve months, is often given out by the health visitor at a baby's eight-month check. The books come in a canvas bag which contains two board books and a book of nursery rhymes, along with information on sharing books and how to join the library. Currently two additional packs are given out in England – Bookstart Plus for 18-month-olds and My Bookstart Treasure Chest, which is aimed at three-year-olds.

From an early age your baby will be happy to sit looking at books with you, especially ones which she can touch and feel.

Your older baby will like having a selection of books and will be able to enjoy looking at the pictures.

Week 20

Your baby's progress

You'll have noticed changes in your baby's physical abilities each week, but now he has reached five months old, these changes are likely to be more noticeable than ever. He is likely to be concentrating his efforts on practising his head control. Watch for him lifting his head and shoulders off the floor while he's lying on his back. This is good exercise for strengthening his neck muscles, which he needs to do so that he can sit up unsupported. If you hold him lightly in a sitting position you'll be able to feel his muscles tense as he attempts to balance on his own.

Your baby is also adding new sounds to his vocabulary and will now be concentrating on one-syllable words such as 'ba' or 'ma', which he will repeat over and over again. This use of early speech is known as babbling and is not really a form of communication, but rather a way of exploring new sounds. It may drive you crazy, but he is likely to practise this sound over and over again for hours on end before he moves on to a new one.

Socially your baby is beginning to show response to others, especially you, in a number of different ways. He may indicate that he is happy to see you by squealing, laughing, waving his arms and legs, smiling or cooing. You can encourage this interaction by talking to your baby and playing games with him.

Your baby will enjoy sitting up for short periods. Support his back by either holding him or propping him with cushions.

Parents' survival guide

Mums

If you haven't already done so, now is a good time to take up some form of exercise. It doesn't have to be too strenuous, or take up a lot of your time, but it does need to be regular and should be carried out for an hour at least twice a week. You could try brisk walking, or jogging with your baby if you have a suitable pushchair. Alternatively, you could join a gym that has crèche facilities, or go to an exercise class while your partner or someone else you trust looks after your baby. Whatever you do, make sure it's a form of exercise that you enjoy as this will give you the incentive to keep going.

Dads

It may be time for a night out, just the two of you. If close family are not available, you'll need to find a good alternative for babysitting duties. The best way to do this is by word-of-mouth, but if that's not an option you may have to join a babysitting circle, go to an agency or follow up an advertisement. Ideally, a babysitter should be over 16 years and should have basic childcare skills like nappy-changing and a reasonable knowledge of first aid. Make sure you leave her all your contact details as well as the phone number for your doctor and local hospital. If your babysitter is unknown to you, always check her references.

Milestones for week 20

Your baby...

* may be able to lift up his head and shoulders when lying on his back
* can sit for a short time if his back is supported
* may attempt to balance on his own when held in a sitting position
* is adding new sounds to his vocabulary and may be saying one-syllable words
* loves repetition and will enjoy doing the same thing over and over again.

You...

* should be taking some form of exercise for an hour at least twice a week
* need to spend time outside in the fresh air each day with your baby
* may want to find a regular babysitter or join a baby-sitting circle.

Teething

Although there is no fixed time for your baby to start teething, on average a baby's first tooth appears some time between now and seven months. However, it's thought that tooth eruption follows hereditary patterns, so if you or your partner went through the teething process especially early or late your baby is likely to do the same.

Some babies produce teeth without any difficulty, while others seem to suffer a lot of discomfort and become miserable and upset each time a tooth starts to come through. Teething symptoms often precede the tooth itself by several weeks, or in some cases months, and vary from child to child.

Drooling or dribbling is often the first sign that teeth are on their way and this can start as early as ten weeks. Excessive drooling can cause a skin rash or chapping of the skin around the mouth and on the chin. Keeping your baby's skin dry and treating the affected area with a mild skin cream should solve the problem.

Biting is another indication of teething and your baby may start to bite on anything he can get into his mouth, including your fingers. Chewing on hard objects helps to relieve the pressure under the gums, so giving your baby a chilled teething ring or a slice of carrot (if he's started taking solids) may bring some relief. Alternatively you can try gently massaging his gums with a clean finger or rubbing on a teething gel.

Ear-pulling and cheek-rubbing may also be signs of teething, as pain can travel along nerve paths to these areas. This is common when molars start to come through. If your baby is over three months you can give him the recommended dose of paracetamol suspension (if he's under three months you will need to ask your health visitor for advice).

It used to be thought that fever, earache or diarrhoea were also signs of teething but it's now accepted that this isn't the case, so if your baby has any of these illnesses while teething you may want to seek medical advice.

lateral incisor

upper incisor

canine

first molar

3 2 2 3

upper jaw

second molar

second molar

lower jaw

canine

first molar

4 1 1 4

lower incisor

lateral incisor

This chart displays the order in which your baby's teeth will probably appear.

Keeping teeth clean

As soon as the first tooth appears you will need to start taking care of your baby's oral hygiene. You'll probably find it easiest to clean these first teeth using your finger, wrapped in a soft cloth. Once your baby has got used to the idea you will be able to progress to a soft baby toothbrush with a pea-sized blob of toothpaste – choose one that has been specially formulated for children. Make teeth cleaning fun by encouraging your baby to try cleaning his own teeth once you've finished brushing them.

Some babies grow teeth without any signs of discomfort while others seem to suffer quite a bit.

Baby massage

Touch is an important part of your child's physical and emotional growth, and massage is an ideal way of extending your natural inclination to caress and cuddle your baby. You'll find that massage has other health benefits for your baby, too, such as alleviating wind, relieving colic and generally aiding his digestive system. It can also help to make your baby's developing muscles stronger and more supple.

For massage to be successful you need to choose a time when you and your baby are both calm and relaxed, perhaps half an hour after his feed or when he's had his bath. Your baby will need to be naked, so before you begin, check that the room is warm – at least 26 °C (78 °F) – and draught-free. You'll need a soft surface for your baby to lie on so that he is feeling comfortable and secure.

Before you begin, remove any jewellery that could scratch your baby and make sure that your fingernails are short, with no jagged edges. Relax your hands by stretching and shaking them, then warm them up by rubbing them together. Place a small amount of baby oil or olive oil in your hands and start gently massaging your baby's skin using light, rhythmic movements. The massage should flow from your baby's head to his face, then his chest, shoulders, arms, stomach and legs, finishing with his feet.

Talk quietly to your baby while you massage him, keeping your face close to his and looking into his eyes. This will help to make this a very personal and pleasurable experience for you both. Ideally the massage should last for five to ten minutes – any longer and your baby will probably get bored. When you've finished and he is dressed, allow him to go to sleep if that is what he seems to want.

Sometimes your baby will make it obvious that he doesn't want to cooperate, and when this happens don't attempt to force him. It's better to stop immediately and then try again another time.

Your baby will need to be on a soft surface so that she feels warm and comfortable while you massage her.

Massage techniques

Even if massage is new to you, don't be afraid to try it on your baby. Stroking and touching can be a pleasurable experience for you both and will help strengthen the bond between you.

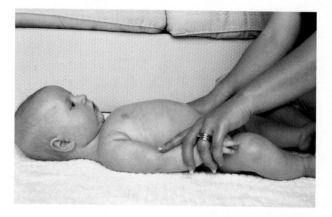

1 Once you've massaged your baby's head, place both hands on his chest then, using gentle, firm strokes, massage upwards and outwards across his shoulders and down his arms to his hands.

If you are worried about how to perform a massage your health visitor should be able to give you basic guidance. Some health visitors run special baby-massage courses, or you could see if there are any privately run courses in your area.

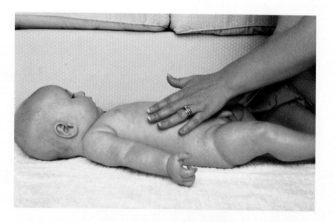

2 Starting below the ribcage, gently massage your baby's abdomen, using a circular movement in a clockwise direction.

Newborn babies

Your newborn baby is likely to respond well to gentle massage, but remember to use only your fingertips so that your touch is light and extremely gentle.

You will also need to be extra careful when stroking over the fontanelles (soft spots) on his head and around his still-healing navel. A newborn naturally reverts to the foetal position when you lie him down so you will have to work around this without trying to straighten out his arms and legs.

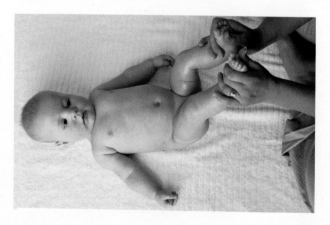

3 Begin at your baby's thighs, then massage down the length of his legs until you reach his feet. Now gently caress his toes and then apply circular movements to each heel.

Week 21

Your baby's progress

Your baby is busy learning about what's happening in the world around her and will probably be fascinated by everyday objects that look different and do different things to the toys she's become used to. Offer her some household items to play with, such as a wooden spoon, and show her how to bang it so that it makes a noise. Put some dried pasta in a sealed plastic container and show her how she can make a different type of noise by shaking it.

She is still putting everything into her mouth to test what it feels like. This 'mouthing' also helps her find out whether something tastes good, what temperature it is and even whether it's edible or not. It's her way of learning about the properties of different objects and is an important part of her development, but do make sure that she can't get hold of objects that she could choke on such as coins or small parts of a toy.

Your baby will probably enjoy standing and bouncing up and down on your knees. This is a great form of exercise that will help strengthen her legs ready for crawling and, eventually, walking. If you haven't already introduced her to a baby bouncer, now might be a good time.

Sitting up on her own is another skill your baby is trying to master. She'll enjoy sitting propped up, supported by cushions, even though she is likely to topple over if she tries to get at something out of reach. Don't rush to pick her up immediately this happens – watch what she does. She may manage to manoeuvre herself into a position where she can reach the item she wants and play with it.

Help strengthen your baby's legs by holding him in a standing position on your lap and letting him push his legs against you.

Parents' survival guide

Mums

Your life will probably have settled into a routine now that your baby is more predictable. This should mean that you can plan ahead a bit more, which should allow you some time to yourself. Perhaps you could have a girlie lunch with friends from work, or a trip to the beauty salon for a bit of pampering, or maybe you just want to go window shopping or read a book uninterrupted. The important thing is that whatever you choose to do makes you feel good.

Find someone you trust to look after your baby for a couple of hours each week. Perhaps you could take turns at looking after each other's babies with another mum from the parent and baby group, or maybe you have a relative who'll be more than happy to stay with your baby while you are out. Even if these aren't an option for you, your partner should be able to look after your baby for a while each week.

Dads

Your baby should have you wound round her little finger by now. She's at a stage when she's most responsive to the people she knows and likes best, which will be you and your partner. Enjoy being one of the two most important people in her world and try to spend as much one-to-one time as you can with her.

Milestones for week 21

Your baby...

* will enjoy pushing with her legs so that she bounces up and down
* uses her mouth to test the temperature and properties of different items
* may try to sit up unaided
* can probably roll over in both directions now
* continues to practise her talking skills by repeating single-syllable words such as 'da' and 'ma'.

You...

* need to check that your baby's toys are safe with no small or broken parts she could choke on
* could buy or borrow a baby bouncer to see if your baby enjoys it
* might want to invest in a new 'pick-me-up' hair style or colour.

Swimming classes

Swimming is the only activity which allows your baby to be completely independent before she has even begun to crawl or walk. Because water supports her weight it enables her to move freely, so that when she's swimming she can make completely different movements to those she practises normally. There's no need to worry about her going under the water – all babies are born with a diving reflex which means that they naturally hold their breath when submerged. This reflex lasts until they are around 18 months old.

Your baby can start swimming classes from as early as a few weeks old, although at this age she will need to go to a pool where the water is extra-warm. For babies under three months or weighing less than 5.5 kg (12 lb 2 oz) the water temperature should be 32 °C (90 °F); 30 °C (86 °F) will suffice for babies older than this. Never let your baby get cold. If she starts to shiver, remove her from the pool immediately and wrap her in a towel.

Although some classes prefer babies to have had all their vaccinations before they start there is actually no reason why babies can't go swimming before they've been immunised. The chlorine in the pool protects against the risk of infection. For more information check out the NHS website www.immunisation.org.uk.

Always check out the pool and the qualifications of the instructor before you sign up for a class. Look for a pool where the temperature for these classes is guaranteed and where a regular check is made on the level of the chemicals used in the water. The instructor should have a life-saving certificate, and preferably a Red Cross Mother and Baby certificate. Finally, make sure that there are no more than ten babies in the class. If there are more than this you're unlikely to get the attention that you need to make these classes a success.

The majority of specialist swimming classes have a clear and progressive structure for their users. Some will incorporate underwater swimming, which is thought to further enhance the development of muscle tone and strength, coordination and cardiovascular fitness, while others put more emphasis on just having fun. The most important thing is that no one ever tries to force your baby to do something that you and she are not happy with.

If you decide to take your baby to the local pool on your own, use the baby pool until your child is four months old – this is warmer and less frightening for a young baby. Once you progress to the adult pool you'll need to keep the sessions short – around ten minutes at first, building to no more than 30 minutes. It's best to go at off-peak times, when the pool is likely to be quieter. During your first few sessions you'll need to keep your face close to your baby's and maintain eye contact so that she feels safe. Later, when she has more confidence, you'll be able to move her further away from you and she'll enjoy being swished around in the water.

Whether you go to organised classes or your local pool, your baby will need a swim nappy as well as a towel in which to wrap her as soon as she comes out of the water. Swimming can make babies hungry, so be prepared to feed her after her swim.

Some babies take time and a little coaxing to relax in the water, while others take to it immediately.

Swimming benefits

The main benefits for your baby are:
❄ it allows free movement and improves core muscle development and coordination
❄ it helps to strengthen the heart, lungs and respiratory system
❄ if done regularly, it can improve eating and sleeping patterns
❄ it is a great life skill.

Plus for you, some benefits are:
❄ it can be great bonding activity for dads and babies
❄ it's fun and socially stimulating
❄ it's a good way to meet other mums with young babies.

Week 22

Your baby's progress

Your baby now has the strength to hold up his head and neck while pushing himself up so that his shoulders and chest are clear of the floor. It won't be long now before he can lift up his tummy and manoeuvre his legs and feet until he's in a position to crawl forwards or shuffle backwards.

Your baby's grasp is becoming more coordinated so that he is now capable of holding an object with one hand and reaching out and taking a second object with the other hand. He is also able to transfer an object successfully from one hand to the other. You'll notice that he is beginning to use his fingers individually now rather than grasping with his whole hand.

Your baby has been fascinated with mirrors from an early age. He will enjoy looking at himself in the mirror and may even amuse himself by pulling faces and attempting to touch his reflection. Your baby is beginning to work out that the person he sees in the mirror is in fact himself. You can help him to establish this recognition by looking in the mirror with him so that he sees you beside him. Your face is probably the one that your baby recognises most easily, so seeing himself and you together in the mirror will help him to develop a sense of his individual identity.

Your baby should be able to lift his head and shoulders off the floor quite easily now, and may even be manoeuvring himself backwards and forwards, demonstrating his growing strength and muscle control.

Parents' survival guide

Mums

Deciding whether or not to return to full-time work can be a very difficult decision. Some women can't bear the thought of leaving their babies and would rather live on a reduced income than return to work; some miss the stimulation of the workplace and feel that they will be a better parent if they themselves are more satisfied; others have no choice but to return to work.

Part-time work can be the answer for many women, and the good news is that parents of children under the age of six have the right to apply for more flexible working hours and your employer has to consider such a request seriously. Before you approach your employer it's a good idea to think through just how this would work. If you can present the idea in such a way that it can be seen to have benefits for you both, it is much more likely to be viewed favourably. You can find out more about flexible working on the Department of Trade and Industry website, www.dti.gov.uk or call the Acas Helpline, 08457 47 47 47, and ask for their advice leaflet.

Dads

Now may be a good time to look at your finances, especially if your partner has decided not to return to work. A independent financial advisor (IFA) will be able to suggest how to make the most of your income; contact the Association of Independent Financial Advisors on www.aifa.net for a list of advisors in your area.

If you haven't already done so, you and your partner should make a will which includes details of the people you would want to be your baby's guardians should anything happen to you. Although you can do a DIY will, it's better to use a solicitor. Ask friends if they can recommend one, look in your telephone directory under solicitor, or contact your local Citizens Advice Bureau for help. Alternatively, the Law Society will give you a list of solicitors in your area, and you'll find lots of useful information on their website, www.lawsociety.org.uk.

Milestones for week 22

Your baby...

✿ may be able to do push ups with his arms so that he lifts his head, shoulders and upper chest up off the floor
✿ will perhaps be able to shuffle himself across the floor
✿ begins to show signs of self-awareness
✿ is beginning to understand object permanence.

You...

✿ may love every moment you spend at home with your baby, or may be missing adult company. Both feelings are quite normal
✿ could perhaps have one evening a week when you go out with friends while your partner looks after the baby.

Mixed feeding

If you're returning to work you will need to think about how your baby will be fed when you are away from her. If you're breastfeeding you may wish to continue for as long as possible and going back to work shouldn't stop you. There's no reason why you can't continue to give your baby breast milk exclusively if you express milk and store it so that it can be given to your baby in a bottle (*see* p.86) during the day, while you breastfeed in the mornings, evenings and at weekends.

Alternatively, you may find it easier to introduce mixed feeding so that you breastfeed when you're at home and your baby's carer gives her formula milk when you are not. If you've been exclusively breastfeeding up until now

you will need to reduce the number of feeds you give your baby gradually, or your breasts are likely to become uncomfortable. It takes your breasts three to seven days to adjust to missing one feed, so aim to drop one a week, starting well before you return to work.

At first it may be easier to get your partner or carer to offer the bottle to your baby so that she doesn't become confused by the smell of your breast milk and the different taste of formula. Sucking from a teat is a different action from sucking on the breast and your baby will need to learn this, too, if she's never been bottle fed before. Some babies take to the change without any difficulty, while others refuse the bottle at first but eventually learn to accept it.

Combined feeding doesn't always work and you may find that your baby chooses the bottle over your breast because sucking on a teat is easier for her than breastfeeding. If you find that your milk supply is deteriorating because she prefers the bottle, you could try having a weekend where you only breastfeed her. This should increase your milk supply again. Whatever you do, don't allow this to become a battle between you as this can be an emotional time for you, especially if you are returning to work and leaving her for long periods for the first time. You should not feel that you've failed if you cannot manage combined feeding – you've breastfed her for as long a time as you could and have given her the best possible start in life.

Breastfeeding is the best and most natural way to feed your baby and breastmilk has the added advantage of always being available.

How can you help?

Bottle feeding

Feeding from a bottle uses a different technique to feeding from the breast, and you may find that your baby takes a little time to become accustomed to this new method. You can help her by:

❋ introducing the bottle when she is neither starving hungry nor completely full

❋ feeding her somewhere different to where you usually sit, so that she doesn't associate bottle feeding with the normal breastfeeding routine

❋ feeding her in the dark, so she can't see the bottle

❋ warming the teat before offering it to her.

Week 23

Your baby's progress

Your baby's first forward movements are likely to occur at any time now. He will be able to push or drag himself a few centimetres across the floor by using his arms and legs in a frog-like motion. You can help him by keeping your hands placed against the bottom of his feet to act as leverage as he straightens his legs to push himself across the floor. It won't be long before he'll be able to do this without your help.

His ability to sit up will have noticeably progressed as well and he may now be able to sit for longer periods with only a small cushion for support. You will notice that his head is steadier and that he can keep his back muscles tensed for longer so that his balance in this position is improved.

Your baby learns a lot about his environment through his hands and his sense of touch. His tactile awareness is becoming more sophisticated so that he can now tell whether something is hot or cold, rough or smooth and wet or dry. Giving him the opportunity to touch a wide range of objects with varied textures will help him to develop this skill further.

Put a collection of everyday objects in a bag – such as a feather, a piece of cotton wool, a teaspoon and a woolly glove – and encourage your baby to put his hands into the bag and pull each item out. Watch his face as he discovers how different each object feels.

You may notice that your baby is showing more interest in his toys now. Rather than just picking them up and shaking them or putting them in his mouth, he will actually look at them as he manipulates them. Offer a variety of toys with different properties to give him plenty to explore.

Unusual objects will hold great interest for your baby now. Items such as car keys will make a satisfying sound when he shakes them, and different shapes will fascinate him.

Parents' survival guide

Mums

If you are a single parent you may be finding this time very difficult, especially if you haven't got the support of family living nearby. It's easy to feel isolated and lonely, as single friends from your pre-baby life may not understand the changes you have had to make since your baby arrived. Try to keep in touch and make some space for them in your life, even if it's only for the occasional coffee together. Good friendships are important, especially if the going gets tough.

You may find your best support comes from other single parents who understand what you are going through. Your health visitor may be able to put you in touch with a local group or you can contact Gingerbread, a self-help organisation for single parents with groups all over the country (www.gingerbread.org.uk), where you will find friendship and practical advice, too. Alternatively, the National Council for One Parent Families have produced a Lone Parent Handbook which covers just about everything you need to know on a practical level. Their website, www.oneparentfamilies.org.uk, is also packed with useful information and tips.

Recent statistics show that one in four women experience domestic violence at some point in their lives, with 30 per cent taking place during pregnancy or after the birth. The abuse can take many forms – physical, sexual, emotional and psychological abuse are all considered to be domestic violence. If this is happening to you then it's vital that you talk to your doctor or health visitor so they can help.

Dads

Domestic violence doesn't just affect women. New statistics show that one man in every six will suffer from domestic violence at some point in their lives, although only 19 per cent of these men will publicly admit to having been abused. If domestic violence is an issue for you, contact Mankind at www.mankind.org.uk or ring their helpline: 0870 794 4192. If you're a single dad you can get help and support from other single fathers on www.dads-uk.co.uk.

Milestones for week 23

Your baby...

✤ may show an increased awareness of himself and his surroundings
✤ is learning about cause and effect by repeating actions over and over again
✤ is starting to show that he can remember things
✤ continues to 'babble' but in a modified tone so that it sounds more like real speech.

You...

✤ and your partner may want to consider the roles of chief carer and breadwinner and discuss the idea of role reversal
✤ will need to check out your wardrobe if you are returning to work soon.

Signing

This is a sign language that parents can use with their babies before they can talk. Introduced from the USA, signing is based on a series of basic symbols which allow your baby to communicate with you. Although your baby is capable of learning signs from six months onwards, it may be a couple of months before he starts signing back because he has to have developed the ability to recognise, remember and then make the signs before he can start using them.

Since the American child-development researcher Joseph Garcia first came up with the idea of baby signing, it has taken off both in the USA and in the UK so that you can now find signing organisations and groups all over the country. Although there are different interpretations of how signing should be done – some organisations use the British Sign Language (BSL) signs, while others encourage parents and babies to develop their own signs – the principle on which signing is based is the same. (The argument for using BSL signs is that anyone who knows this sign language can then sign with your baby.) Some classes combine signing with music, so parents and babies come together to sing songs, join in musical activities and learn a range of simple signs.

The idea is that your baby uses simple hand signals to tell you what he wants or needs, for example that he's hungry, wants more milk, is tired and so on. You teach him the signs by using them appropriately, so when you give him his milk you sign 'milk', and when something is too hot you sign 'hot'. It's best to start with a few basic signs and then build up your repertoire as your baby progresses.

There is a concern among some experts that using sign language will reduce the amount of time parents spend talking and listening to their babies. They feel that most parents instinctively know what their baby wants – even if it takes a

little while to work it out – without having to resort to signing. However, people who believe that signing is of real benefit to parents and babies say that signing makes the communication process faster and therefore avoids frustration, which leads to calmer, happier babies.

There is certainly no evidence to suggest that signing has a detrimental effect on a baby – in fact some researchers suggest that it gives babies a head start in life, especially with talking. Babies who learn to sign often start to talk earlier and develop their vocabulary faster.

For more information about signing, contact www.babysigners. co.uk, tel: 01273 882203. To find out about signing and singing groups, contact www.singandsign.com (tel: 01273 550587) or www.tinytalk.co.uk (tel: 0870 2424 898).

Signing basics

* Begin with simple words such as 'milk', 'eat', 'hot' and 'cold'.
* Follow your baby's lead and introduce signs that describe things that are important to him.
* Always say the word you are signing.
* Only use one sign per sentence.
* Be consistent in the signs that you use.
* Keep calm and relaxed about signing so that it's fun.

Signing classes teach a baby to use simple hand signals to communicate his needs.

Mobility

All babies go through the same stages of mobility, starting with the head and working down to the feet, but how fast they progress from one stage to another varies considerably. Each baby is different and yours will do things at his own pace. He has to be able to hold his head up before he can sit upright or crawl, and he needs to be able to crawl or bottom shuffle before he can walk. He also has to learn to control his arms and legs before he's able to gain control of his hands and feet.

As a newborn, your baby has no control whatsoever over his head, which flops around if you don't support it. As his neck muscles become stronger you'll see your baby lifting his head and holding it for a few seconds before letting it drop down again. By three months he'll probably be able to hold his head up quite steadily.

The next stage of mobility comes when your baby starts to roll around, first from side to back, and then a few weeks later from back to side. At first the movement is accidental, but then it becomes a way of practising control over his body, so your baby will do it over and over again. He soon realises that rolling lets him view his world from different angles and can be used to get him closer to something he wants.

Your baby will begin to practise shuffling around on the floor at around seven months, using the newfound strength in his neck and shoulders.

Between six and ten months, your baby may begin to crawl, or at least attempt to get into crawling position.

At around four months your baby will be able to lift his head, shoulders, arms and legs off the floor when you put him down on his front. This new 'swimming' movement is his way of getting ready to crawl. By six to seven months your baby may be able to support himself in a crawling position, although he won't be going anywhere just yet. It'll be a few more weeks before he's learnt to control his movements well enough to propel himself either forwards or backwards. Once he's mastered that he'll be off and it'll be only a matter of time before he pulls himself up onto his feet using you or the furniture for support.

At some time around one year he'll have gained enough confidence to let go and walk on his own. These first steps will be very wobbly and ungainly, with bent legs and feet placed wide apart to help him balance. With a bit of practice his legs will straighten and he'll become steadier on his feet.

Sitting requires a different set of movements and it'll be around nine months before your baby sits by himself and can reach in front, upwards, to the side and behind without falling over. Being able to control his sitting-down movement won't happen until he's eleven to twelve months old – until then, when he wants to sit down from standing he'll simply let go and land on his bottom on the floor.

Safety tips

❋ **Don't** use a baby walker because of the risk of accidents.

❋ **Don't** be in a hurry to put your baby in shoes – he doesn't need them until he's running about outside.

How can you help?

Getting to his feet

There are many ways that you can help your baby to walk:

❋ encourage him to stand on your knee and bounce up and down to strengthen his legs

❋ let him spend short periods of time in a baby bouncer

❋ once he can sit upright, place toys slightly out of his reach so that he has to reach for them

❋ hold a toy behind him in order to encourage him to twist around

❋ give him some push-along toys to encourage him to crawl and walk.

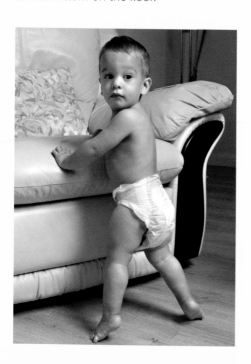

At about nine months your baby will be able to pull himself up to a standing position and start to 'cruise' around the furniture.

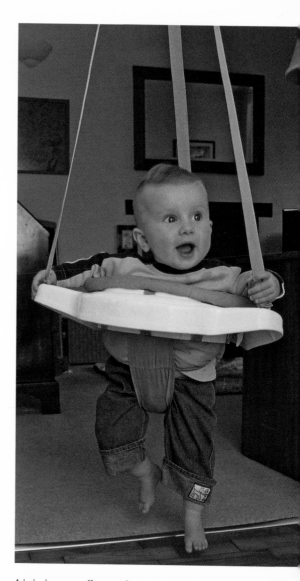

A baby bouncer offers good exercise for strengthening the muscles in a baby's legs, and in an upright position your baby can watch you as you move around the room.

Week 24

Your baby's progress

Your baby's ability to reach and hold will probably have developed noticeably over the past few weeks. Now she can reach up and down as well as straight ahead and to the side. When she grasps an object she will hold it with the side of her hand and the last two fingers in what's known as the 'palmar grasp'. She also has more control over her hand and arm movements now, so that rather than flap them around as she did when she was younger she now moves them in a smoother, more coordinated manner.

Although your baby is too young to use words to describe what she does or doesn't want, her ability to communicate through gestures is beginning to develop. Watch for her holding out her arms when she wants to be picked up, or feel how she hangs on tightly when she doesn't want you to put her down. By responding to these early gestures you are telling your baby that you understand and are responding to what she's trying to tell you.

The attachment your baby has for you is obvious from the way she behaves if you leave her and the excitement she shows when you return. She may become clingy and refuse to go to another adult, even one she knows well if she suspects you are about to leave her. She's likely to fuss and cry when you do leave her, but this will soon pass. A certain wariness of strangers is quite natural at this age. Don't try to force your child to go to someone that she seems wary of.

Play hand games with your baby to encourage him to develop his hand and arm control.

Parents' survival guide

Mums

If you are putting your baby into a nursery or using a registered childminder, ask your employer about the Childcare Voucher scheme. This is a scheme supplied by some employers to working parents that will save you a significant amount of money on your childcare over a year. A child qualifies for the scheme up to 1 September following their fifteenth birthday (or 1 September following their sixteenth birthday if the child is disabled).

To be able to use these vouchers your child must be looked after by a registered or approved childcare provider. To find out if a childcare provider is registered or approved you'll need to ask for their approval number, or for a copy of their certificate. To check the details you can telephone Ofsted direct on 0845 601 4771, check out www.faircare.co.uk or call the Fair Care helpline on 0870 777 0711. If your baby is being cared for in your own home by a relative you won't be able to use Childcare Vouchers. However, a relative looking after your baby alongside other unrelated children in their own home can qualify, provided they become registered or approved.

Dads

Men are also eligible for the Childcare Voucher scheme, so find out from your employer whether such a scheme exists in your company or whether they would consider running one. If you are married, or you and your partner live together and have shared parental responsibility for your child, and you are both working, then you can both take part in the scheme, which means you double your entitlement.

Milestones for week 24

Your baby...

❋ will take her cues from you about things that cause her anxiety. If you are reassuring, then she'll be happier about accepting a new object or situation

❋ can let you know with gestures what she does or doesn't want

❋ may babble one syllable in a sentence-like form such as 'ba-ba-ba-ba'

❋ continues to practise her pre-crawling movements.

You...

❋ may need to finalise your childcare arrangements if you are returning to work soon

❋ might want to have a practice run at the journey between the childminder or nursery and the office to check on timings

❋ could consider (if you have decided to remain at home) exchanging a few hours' childcare with another mum so that you both get a few hours to yourselves each week.

Safety around the home

Safety first

Once your baby starts to reach out for things and to move around on her own you will need to pay a great deal of attention to her safety. Even at this early age she could wriggle or roll into a hazardous situation and her natural tendency to put everything into her mouth can be an added risk.

Your baby will continue to develop fast, so that things she may not be able to reach now will be within her grasp before you realise it. Any new mobility could lead her into new dangers, so it is a good idea to look at every room from floor level before putting her down to play and kick. This way you can often spot hazards such as uncovered sockets which could have things poked into them, or loose threads at the edge of a rug on which she could choke.

There is a wide range of equipment you can buy to help make your home safer. Some of the most useful items are listed here in the safety equipment boxes. In some areas councils offer free safety equipment to parents on certain benefits, so it's worth asking your health visitor what's available. However, remember that equipment on its own isn't enough – it's your vigilance that really counts.

Hall, stairs and living rooms

These areas are often difficult to keep safe because the environment constantly changes as people come in and out and items are moved. You'll need to make frequent safety checks as your child grows and becomes more mobile. Falling down the stairs is very common when a baby is not yet steady but wants to be independent. Never leave your child unattended near the stairs.

Making a home safe

What you can do to ensure a safe home:

* ensure that there is no loose floor covering or any trailing wires at the top of the stairs that you could trip on while carrying your baby

* check that the gaps between banisters are no more than 10 cm (4 in) so that your baby can't get her head stuck between them

* cover over any horizontal landing railings to prevent your baby from falling through them

* check that the lighting is good so that there is no risk of tripping on some unseen object on the stairs

* cover unused electrical sockets so that your baby can't poke anything into the holes

* make sure that there are no sharp corners on any furniture that your baby could hurt herself on

* place ornaments and breakables out of reach

* use mats instead of tablecloths so that your baby can't pull things off the table

Safety equipment

* Fix safety gates at the top and bottom of the stairs. It is important to follow the manufacturer's instructions.
* Place smoke alarms throughout the house. They should comply with BS 5446 and you should check them regularly.
* Use fireguards with all fires and heaters. If possible, secure the guard to the wall.
* Use electrical plug socket covers in unused sockets.
* Fit safety corner cushions to tables and cupboards.
* Use a video lock.

✿ check the floor regularly for small objects that your baby could swallow or choke on

✿ keep matches and lighters well out of reach

✿ always make sure your child's bouncer, walker or rocker is placed well away from anything that could be pulled or grabbed

✿ never place your baby in a bouncing cradle on a raised surface as she could easily fall off

✿ never have hot or alcoholic drinks where your baby can reach them

✿ never leave your baby alone in a room where there is an open fire

✿ unplug electric fires when not in use.

A child safety gate prevents your baby from gaining access to the stairs, deterring potential falls. It can also be used to keep dogs downstairs, away from your baby's nursery.

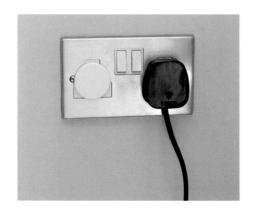

Plug sockets are easy for babies to reach, so make sure that unused sockets are covered to prevent your baby poking small objects into the holes.

Place smoke alarms near the kitchen and your baby's nursery, and regularly check the batteries to make sure that they are working.

A safe kitchen

With hot hobs and oven doors, boiling liquids in saucepans, sharp knives and other utensils, and probably cleaning chemicals stored in a floor-level cupboard too, the kitchen is probably the most potentially dangerous room in a house for a inquisitive child and is no place for a baby unless she is strapped securely into a highchair. Where possible, install a safety gate or barrier to keep your child out altogether. If this is not an option then you should do all

you can to ensure that, when she is in the kitchen, she is kept safe:

❋ make sure your baby can't get into the kitchen without you knowing

❋ put all sharp objects, such as knives, well out of reach

❋ keep the flex from any appliances out of reach of your baby and, if possible, use a cordless kettle and iron

❋ cook on the back rings of the hob with the pan handles facing inwards

❋ make sure that all household chemicals and cleaning materials are locked away. Buy products with child-resistant lids

❋ keep the doors of electrical appliances such as washing machines and tumble-dryers closed and unplug when not in use.

Safety equipment

❋ Fit safety catches to all low-level cupboards and drawers, the refrigerator and the freezer.
❋ Fit safety locks to your dishwasher, tumble dryer and washing machine.
❋ Keep a fire blanket or an extinguisher near the cooker in case of emergencies.

Replace all door handles on low-level kitchen cupboards with round-edged knobs so that your baby can't hurt herself. Fix safety catches so that your baby can't open the doors without you noticing.

Bathroom safety

The most common accidents in the bathroom are falls on wet surfaces, scalds and burns from water that's too hot, poisoning from bathroom cleaning products and medicines, and even cuts from sharp objects such as a razor. To ensure you keep the bathroom as safe as possible:

✤ keep all medicines and dangerous objects, such as a razor, locked away in a cabinet

✤ use a non-slip mat in the bottom of the bath to prevent your baby from slipping

✤ hang a towel over the taps to prevent your child burning herself

✤ keep the toilet brush out of reach

✤ keep the thermostat turned down to 46 °C (115 °F) to avoid your child being scalded by the hot tap water

✤ if you have a heated towel rail, turn it down thermostatically to 46 °C (115 °F).

Never leave your baby unattended at bath time, and always support her neck and head so that she doesn't slip under the water.

Safety equipment

✤ Fit a lock to the toilet seat.

✤ Fix locks to the windows.

✤ Use a door jammer to prevent your child shutting herself in the bathroom.

✤ Place a tap guard over the taps.

A safe nursery

Your baby is nearly old enough now to leave your bedroom and start sleeping in the nursery. However, even if you decide to keep her with you for a while and you are using the nursery just to change and dress her, regular safety checks will be needed in this area too as she grows increasingly mobile and adventurous. Here's what you can do to keep her safe:

❉ put in a nursery light, dimmer switch or plug light so that you can check on your baby without disturbing her

❉ install a nursery listening device so that you can continually monitor your baby

❉ place the cot away from the window

❉ place a thermometer in the nursery to keep a check on the temperature so that your baby doesn't become overheated. The correct temperature is around 18 °C (65 °F)

❉ never leave your baby alone on a raised surface as she could easily roll off it onto the floor

❉ always put your baby down in her cot if you have to leave her alone for a few minutes while you're in the nursery.

Put your baby's changing mat on the floor so that there is no chance of her hurting herself if she rolls off.

Cover sharp corners on furniture so your baby can't hurt herself.

Safety equipment

❉ Fit window locks, even if the nursery is on the ground floor.

❉ Fix a smoke alarm outside your baby's room.

❉ Use corner protectors on any sharp corners.

Play safe

Playtime should be an exciting time of fun and learning for your child, but there can still be dangers in a play environment. Falls, cuts and choking are just some of the accidents that could befall her while she is playing.

Always make sure that you check the following before you let your baby commence playing:

❈ toys should be suitable for your baby's age

❈ regularly check all toys for sharp edges or loose bits that could be swallowed

❈ keep push-along and ride-on toys away from stairs and sloping surfaces.

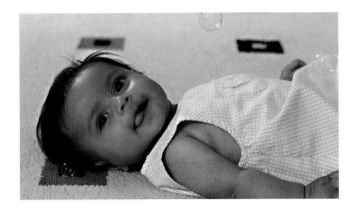

Try blowing bubbles at your baby. She will love tracking the bubbles with her eyes and watching them pop. Keep the liquid out of reach in case your baby tries to drink it.

Safety note

Never buy toys unless they are marked BS 5665 or BS EN71, or bear the CE or Lion Mark.

First aid

Accidents can happen even in the safest homes. In the event of an emergency your first aid kit needs to be well-stocked and easily accessible. It is a good idea to have your doctor's number pinned up near the telephone with the address of your nearest accident and emergency department.

If you don't have easy access to a car, add the numbers of more than one local taxi firm in case you ever need to get to the hospital urgently. Take time to plan what you would do if an emergency happened, such as an accidental injury to your baby or a fire in the home.

Check that all components of a toy are non-toxic and securely fixed to avoid choking.

Learning to talk

Your baby's brain is tuned to pick up the texture, pattern and rhythm of language, and she will pay more attention to voices talking than to any other sounds she hears. She'll listen intensely to you as you chatter away to her, often moving her whole body in rhythm with the sound of the words. Research has shown that at four days old a baby can tell the difference between their native language and a foreign language.

Your baby has to go through distinct stages of development before she can start talking. The development of language skills involves cognitive, social and motor development because she needs to be able to understand and process information and have the ability to communicate, as well as the physical ability to control the dozens of separate muscles which are involved in speech sounds.

All babies are able to cry when they're born; this is their first means of communication. But if you listen to your newborn carefully you will hear that she also makes other noises like little cries or whimpers and breathy burps. While she is making these first noises she will practise using her mouth and tongue by pushing her lips backwards and forwards in a kind of rhythm. As your baby gradually gains control, the noises she makes will become more sophisticated.

By three months your baby will be communicating with gestures as well as different noises. Try raising your eyebrows at her when you speak to her and then watch as she imitates you. This is the first stage of learning about holding a two-way conversation. When you speak to your baby she will wait until you've finished and then make noises back as though holding a conversation

Soft-cloth books offer your baby the opportunity to enjoy books on her own at this age.

with you. If you don't allow her a turn in this dialogue she will probably become frustrated and cry. She'll be using a lot more sounds and will be able to babble and laugh out loud by the time she's about four months. By six months she'll have a good range of repetitive sounds such as 'ma ma' and 'ba ba'.

'Motherese' is a distinct speech pattern instinctively used by adults when they talk to young babies. It involves the use of a high-pitched, rhythmic singsong tone, repeating words in such a way that you capture your baby's attention. Babies respond well to this and will answer you with smiles and gurgles. Talking to your baby will help her acquire language skills, and some researchers suggest that the more one-to-one conversations and early games a baby has the more advanced her language will be by the time she reaches the age of two.

Get talking

The 'Talk to Your Baby' campaign (www.talkto yourbaby.org.uk) is run by the National Literacy Trust. Its aim is to encourage parents to talk to their children from birth in order to help them become good communicators and thus enjoy happier and more successful lives.

How can you help?

Word games

✽ Start talking to your baby from the moment she's born.

✽ Always respond to your baby's attempts at communicating with you.

✽ Don't be embarrassed about using 'motherese'; it's the language your baby likes best.

✽ Be consistent and use the same words for the same thing every time.

✽ Keep your vocabulary simple.

✽ Spend time looking at picture books with your baby.

Combining movement with word games will help your baby to develop her speech.

Week 25

Your baby's progress

If you haven't already started your baby on solids you will need to as soon as he is getting to the age when milk alone won't satisfy his hunger. You'll probably notice that your baby is showing a great interest in your food and in watching other people eating.

For him to be able to eat solids the tongue-thrust reflex he was born with that prevented him from choking needs to have disappeared. You can tell if it has by offering him some food, such as baby rice, and seeing if his tongue pushes it straight back out of his mouth. If it does he isn't ready for solids just yet.

Your baby has already learned to distinguish between bold colours and is now beginning to work out the differences in pastel shades. He can track small objects easily now and may be able to recognise an object after seeing only a part of it. Playing hide and seek with an object is a good way to help him do this.

He now knows his own name and will react when he hears it being said. He needs to hear it often to learn that it belongs to him, so use it in games and include it in songs and nursery rhymes.

Mood swings are a normal occurrence in babies of this age, so be prepared for yours to be all sweetness and light one minute and cross and tearful the next. These mood swings will gradually lessen over time as he learns to control his emotions.

Hand-clapping games that include the use of his name will help your baby understand that his name belongs to him. Now more than ever, your baby will be able to respond to you and communicate effectively with you through game-playing.

Parents' survival guide

Mums

Leaving your baby can be the hardest thing in the world to do. Maybe you're going back to work, or you have the opportunity to go out for the day without your baby. Great as the idea sounds, when it comes to saying 'goodbye' it's quite likely that you'll regret ever having agreed to leave the house, let alone go away for a few hours. This is made even harder if your baby clings and cries when you try to leave him.

The best way to deal with the parting is to make it as quick and relaxed as possible. Don't spend ages kissing and cuddling him and telling him how much you'll miss him – he'll pick up on your anxiety and start to suspect that something is wrong. Try to be firm but kind. Tell him that you are going out and that you'll be back later; explain who is looking after him and how much fun he's going to have with them, then kiss him, say goodbye and leave the room.

Your baby may cry, scream and make a big fuss, or he may have become distracted by the new person in his life and not take much notice. Both will probably upset you, but rest assured that provided your baby is in familiar surroundings with someone he knows who gives him lots of loving attention he'll be fine. Babies have short memory spans and little concept of time, so he won't be counting the hours until you return – in fact it's quite likely that he will hardly miss you at all.

Dads

Have you thought about becoming a stay-at-home dad? These days more and more dads are taking on the role of chief carer to their babies while the mums go back to work. If this is not for you, how about going part-time? This seems to be an option for about a million dads in Britain. Working part-time gives you the opportunity to spend more time with your family while still continuing with your job. Some couples find that if they both work part-time they can juggle the childcare between them, which not only saves them a lot of money but also means that the child has the benefit of being looked after by both his parents.

Milestones for week 25

Your baby...

* will turn his head when he hears his name being spoken
* can often be easily distracted by the introduction of a new game, hand-clapping or a quick change of scene
* may give you hugs and kisses
* can start on solids now if he hasn't already done so.

You...

* will find your baby more fun than ever now as he learns to play simple games with you
* can introduce your baby to more vigorous play
* may need to do a certain degree of financial juggling to cope with the additional cost of your growing baby.

Introducing solids

By the time your baby reaches six months of age he'll need to start eating solid food. Some babies are ready a bit earlier than six months, so if your baby appears to be hungry before this, ask your health visitor about weaning him early. Never introduce solids before four months, no matter how hungry your baby appears to be, because his digestive system isn't mature enough to cope with anything other than breast milk or formula.

Although most babies make it obvious when they are no longer satisfied by milk alone, there are some physical signs that will also indicate clearly that your baby is ready to begin solids. Some of the signs to look out for are listed in the panel shown left.

It's important to remember that up until now your baby has never had anything other than milk, so these first foods are a totally new experience for him. He may not like the taste or texture at first and spit everything you give him straight back out. Alternatively, he may love it and immediately demand more. Both reactions are perfectly normal.

Weaning should be done slowly, starting with a teaspoon or two a day. Your baby still needs to continue with milk feeds, as these first solids are not a source of nourishment, but tasters to accustom him to the idea of eating. He'll cope better if these first foods are smooth, so give him cooked fruit or vegetables, either puréed or mashed, or baby rice mixed with breast milk or formula. Offer the food halfway through a milk feed so that he isn't too hungry or too full to want to try it. Never try to force him to eat something he dislikes. Wait for a week or two and then try the food again.

Ready for solid food?

Your baby is ready to move on to solid food when he:

❋ is able to hold up his head and, when he is sitting on your knee with you holding him, can reach out for something, keeping his shoulders steady

❋ puts his hands and toys deliberately in his mouth to explore new textures and sensations. This is helping to prepare his mouth for the varying textures and tastes of solid food

❋ shows an interest in your food by leaning towards your hand when you are eating, looking at the food, smiling and making sucking, happy noises

❋ seems still to be hungry when he's finished a milk feed

❋ starts waking in the night to be fed when he has previously been sleeping through.

Purée fruits and vegetables in a blender if you want to feed your baby fresh yet easy-to-prepare food. Organic foods will reduce his exposure to pesticides and other chemicals.

Weaning your baby

* Offer lots of different tastes.
* If you use manufactured baby food, make sure it's suitable for your baby's age.
* Never feed your baby straight from the tin or jar. Always decant the food into a bowl.
* Let your baby sit with you to eat so that eating becomes a social time.
* If you give your baby food you've cooked for the rest of the family, remove his portion before adding any seasoning.
* Make up your baby's food in batches and freeze in ice-cube trays so that the frozen cubes can be stored in bags ready for defrosting.

Don't introduce more than one or two new tastes every few days. Once your baby is happy with these you can start mixing different foods together. You'll need to encourage your baby to chew, so offer finger foods such as bread 'soldiers' and pieces of cheese or banana. The consistency of your baby's meals should gradually become lumpier as long as the lumps are soft. Try feeding him mashed potato or carrot, cottage cheese and rice pudding.

Foods to include

Once weaning has been established your baby should be having foods such as the ones listed below from the following food groups every day.

* **Starchy foods** Bread, cereals, rice and potatoes.
* **Dairy products** Cheese, yoghurt and full-fat fromage frais. Cows' milk shouldn't be given before one year, but can be used in small quantities in cooking.
* **Meat and fish** Lean meat, poultry and white fish, or vegetarian alternatives such as pulses and grains. Shellfish isn't suitable for babies.
* **Vegetables** Root vegetables, green beans, broccoli and cauliflower.
* **Fruit** Apples, pears, plums, bananas and apricots. Citrus and berry fruits such as strawberries should be introduced with caution as some babies have an allergic reaction to them.

Foods to avoid

* **Salt** It can overload your baby's immature kidneys. Don't add salt to his food and avoid processed and pre-prepared foods as many of these are high in salt.
* **Sugar** Too much sugar can encourage a sweet tooth, which can lead to tooth decay. Don't add sugar to your baby's food and avoid high-sugar foods such as sweetened desserts.
* **Honey** Occasionally honey contains a type of bacteria that can cause infant botulism, so it shouldn't be offered before one year.
* **Egg whites** These shouldn't be given before eight months. Egg yolks can be given earlier, but need to be thoroughly cooked to avoid the risk of salmonella.
* **Nuts** If there's a history of nut allergy in your family avoid foods containing nuts until your child is at least three years old. Whole nuts shouldn't be given to children under five years because of the risk of choking or inhalation. Peanuts are the most commonly inhaled foreign body and, although they may not give immediate symptoms, they can cause pneumonia later.
* **Low-fat and fat-free products** Your baby needs the calories he'll get from full-fat products until he's at least two years of age.

Milk and baby drinks

The amount of milk that your baby drinks will decrease as his intake of solid food increases. However, he still needs at least 600 ml (1 pt) of breast or formula milk – or follow-on milk if he's over six months – each day. Cows' milk is not suitable as a main drink until after one year, although small quantities may be included in foods in the diet such as custard and sauces. Milk from goats or sheep should not be introduced until after one year and, even then, must be pasteurised or boiled.

Once weaning has been established your baby should be encouraged to drink his milk from a feeding cup at mealtimes rather than taking it from a bottle. By the time your baby has reached a year old it is recommended that bottles are no longer offered at all because of the adverse effect on the development of his teeth.

If your baby seems thirsty you can offer cooled boiled water between feeds. Baby drinks and diluted adult pure fruit juice should only be given at mealtimes and should be offered from a feeder cup rather than a bottle once the first teeth have appeared. Other soft drinks, tea and coffee are unsuitable until your child is much older.

Always sterilise your baby's feeding equipment until he is at least eight months old.

Safety and hygiene tips

❋ Always wash your hands before preparing your baby's food and make sure that all work surfaces and chopping boards are completely clean.

❋ Keep pets out of the kitchen and well away from food you're preparing.

❋ Your baby should have his own feeding utensils and these should be sterilised until he is at least eight months of age.

❋ Always use the freshest ingredients and cook food thoroughly.

❋ Freeze extra portions or store them in the refrigerator for no longer than 24 hours.

❋ Your refrigerator should be 5 °C (40 °F) or below.

❋ Keep food stored in the refrigerator in covered containers.

❋ Never reheat your baby's leftovers.

❋ If microwaving, always stir the food to make sure it's cooked all the way through and check that it's cooled before giving it to your baby.

❋ If using bought food, check the safety seals are intact and do not use any that are past their 'use by' date.

Additional vitamins

If you're still breastfeeding after six months your health visitor may suggest that you give your baby infant vitamin drops, which contain vitamins A, C and D. If your baby is drinking formula milk these vitamins will already have been added to the milk during the manufacturing process. Follow-on milks contain these vitamin plus iron, but many health professionals think they are an unnecessary expense.

Your baby will enjoy the feeling of independence once he has learnt to drink from a feeding cup.

Week 26

Your baby's progress

At this age your baby will enjoy playing by herself, and will often be quite happy simply banging her toys together.

Your baby may appear to favour one hand over the other, but it's still too early to say whether she's going to be right- or left-handed. True right- or left-handedness won't be determined until she reaches two to three years of age.

Although your baby will have doubled her weight by six months, she will probably have grown only 12.5–15 cm (5–6 in) in height. This difference in weight and height is quite normal and will gradually right itself so that, by the time she reaches two years of age, she will be about half her adult height.

Playing a game repeatedly with your baby will help her to understand how the game works and once she does, she will be able to start to express her emotions during play. She'll quickly learn to anticipate actions and become excited when she knows what is about to happen. Be prepared for squeals of delight and lots of laughter. Later she may even instigate a game that she particularly enjoys.

If your baby has shown no signs of teething before now, you will probably find in the next month or so that her first tooth puts in an appearance. Watch out for excessive dribbling and chewing as these are early indicators of a tooth about to come through.

Some time between now and nine months your baby will have her next developmental assessment. You will need to remember that babies develop at their own speed in their own time, so there is no pass or fail at these assessments. Your health visitor or doctor is just checking that there are no problems that need to be addressed.

Parents' survival guide

Mums

You must be amazed at how much your baby has changed since her arrival in the world. Gone is the tiny helpless babe who was totally dependent on you for everything – you now are sharing your life with a little person. You'll already be able to see your baby's character developing, and she may even have started to let you know her likes and dislikes.

The next 26 weeks will be equally rewarding. Imagine how much fun you will have together as she becomes more mobile – she may even have taken her first steps by the time she reaches her first birthday. Her vocabulary will increase too, so although she won't be talking at a year, she's likely to say a few words which actually mean something.

Your baby isn't the only one to have gone through enormous changes. Consider what you have learnt in the past few months, especially if this was your first child. You've become a fully-fledged parent with the skills to prove it.

Dads

Many dads say they prefer their babies when they can respond to them and 'do something'. If you're one of these, you'll be in your element now. Your baby has grown into a responsive, lively little person who is fascinated by everything that's going on around her. If you feel that the last six months have gone quickly, be prepared for the next six to do so, but even faster. Try to make the most of the time you spend together as you watch your baby grow into a confident toddler.

Milestones for week 26

Your baby...

❄ is putting on weight steadily
❄ will have got used to taking solids off a spoon and will start to enjoy different tastes
❄ may have her next developmental check soon
❄ will laugh out loud during playtime
❄ may produce her first tooth.

You...

❄ may want to start changing your baby on a changing mat on the floor as she can now roll over very easily
❄ need to keep a check on her toys to make sure that none of them have loose parts on which she could choke
❄ will need to keep clean any teeth that come through.

Allergies

Once you begin to give your baby solids you'll need to be on the lookout for any allergic reaction to the foods that you've introduced. Although allergies in babies are rare, if anyone in your family has eczema, asthma or hayfever you should introduce the most common allergenic foods one at a time. These are wheat, citrus fruits, eggs, nuts, fish, cows' milk and other dairy products.

You'll recognise an allergic reaction because your baby will probably show physical signs such as wheezing, an itchy rash, eczema or diarrhoea. Rarely, a reaction can be so severe that it becomes life-threatening and the child goes into anaphylactic shock.

Sleeping

By the time your baby is six months old she may be sleeping for ten to twelve hours during the night, as well as having a nap in the morning and afternoon. She shouldn't need feeding during the night now, but you may find that she wakes because of discomfort from teething.

In many cases a child will gradually grow out of a food intolerance, but there are cases when it is caused by a medical condition so that the child will never be able to tolerate the offending food (*see* galactosaemia, opposite).

Although allergies are rare, you should be aware of the signs that could indicate that your baby has an allergy when feeding her new foods.

Although nut allergies affect only one to two per cent of the population, they can be extremely serious. Your baby is most likely to be affected if you have a family history of allergies. Peanut allergy is particularly dangerous for children, so it's best to avoid peanuts and anything containing peanut products such as peanut butter or peanut (ground nut) oil until your child is at least three years old. Always check labels and, if you are unsure of the contents of processed food, avoid it.

If you suspect that your child is allergic to a particular food, talk to your health visitor or doctor. Your child needs a balanced diet so removing a food group, for example dairy products, because you suspect a lactose intolerance, will mean that she is missing out on some vital nutrients. Your health visitor or doctor may decide to send you to a dietician who will be experienced in dealing with your particular dietary problem.

If there is a history of an allergic reaction, such as eczema, you will need to introduce potentially problematic foods one at a time.

Breath holding

Although more common in older babies, breath-holding attacks can occur in children as young as three months. Although they are essentially harmless, these attacks can be very frightening for parents. They can happen if your baby becomes upset and lets out a long wail as she breathes out, but then in her distress neglects to breathe in. She may appear slightly blue and in an extreme case could become floppy and seem to lose consciousness. Your child won't ever actually lose consciousness because the moment she begins to faint she will naturally start breathing again. The best thing you can do is to stay calm and comfort her. Try to remember that your baby will not harm herself and will start breathing again naturally. She may seem subdued and quiet for a little while after an attack. Although there is no treatment, you should tell your health visitor or doctor about these attacks.

Galactosaemia

This is a rare inherited condition where a baby is born with an enzyme missing. This enzyme converts lactose, a sugar found in milk, into glucose and, without it, harmful amounts of lactose accumulate in the body. This can lead to damage of the liver, kidneys and brain as well as the eyes. Symptoms of galactosaemia, which occur soon after birth, include severe jaundice, vomiting and diarrhoea and a failure to gain weight. If galactosaemia is diagnosed the child will be on a milk-free diet for life.

More than one baby?

Coping with more than one baby can be stressful, especially when they are newborn and very tiny. When you have twins or more, the first few weeks at home are bound to be pretty daunting. Looking after two babies who are the same age is definitely harder work than looking after two children of different ages. So forget about the state of the house, and don't worry if you haven't had time to get dressed before midday, just concentrate on keeping your babies happy. When your babies are a bit older and you've managed to establish a routine, you'll find things get easier.

A good network of family and friends can be a great boon when you have one baby, so with two or more it is doubly important. Ask for help and don't be afraid to say what sort of help you need; if the ironing basket is overflowing, ask that your ironing is done for you. Often people want to help but don't like to be seen as interfering, so you may be surprised by the amount of support there is out there. If you haven't got family living nearby, or friends who are around to help, talk to your health visitor. She may have some useful suggestions.

Having twins isn't all about hard work – there is a lot of pleasure to be had from having two babies together. Twins have a special relationship with each other and are able to form a strong bond early on. This ready-made friendship means that they are seldom lonely as there is always a playmate on hand. Twins are not usually as clingy as single babies because they've always had to share and they're used to waiting their turn.

Getting support

The Twins and Multiple Births Association (TAMBA) offers professional support and a range of services to families with twins or other multiple births. You can contact TAMBA on www.tamba.org.uk, tell: 0870 770 3305. They will also give you information about local Twins Clubs, where you can get together with other parents over a cup of coffee. This can be a lifeline if you are feeling under pressure because it not only gets you out of the house but allows you to discuss your concerns with people who've already been through, or are currently going through, what you're experiencing.

Breastfeeding twins

It's perfectly possible to breastfeed twins, although it may take a little time to get into a routine that works for you. You may find that you have to wake one of the babies if the other one wants to feed, but after a while they'll get into the same feeding and sleeping schedule so your life will become easier. Try to get some rest when they are both asleep, regardless of the time of day. You'll probably have to resign yourself to snatching the odd hour here and there until they are older and more settled.

Twins have the advantage over a single baby of having a ready-made friendship and a playmate always on hand.

First aid and emergencies

First aid kit

Every home should have a First Aid kit, and you should also carry a basic kit in the car. You can buy ready-made kits from pharmacies, or you can buy the items separately and store them in an airtight container, out of the reach of children. You should replace items as they are used so that you are always ready for an emergency. Your kit should contain:

* assorted plasters
* cotton wool
* sterile dressings
* steristrips
* gauze and crepe bandages
* triangular bandage
* safety pins
* surgical tape
* scissors
* blunt ended tweezers
* paracetamol suspension
* antiseptic solution or wipes
* calamine lotion
* sting-relief cream
* thermometer
* eye bath
* doctor's telephone number
* details of your nearest A & E department.

✚ What you must know

It's important that you have a basic knowledge of First Aid, as many of the minor accidents that happen to babies and young children occur in the home and can be dealt with immediately by their parents. Ideally you should go on a First Aid course – there are special courses for parents which concentrate on First Aid for babies and toddlers. Your local branches of the British Red Cross and St John Ambulance will be able to tell you about the courses that are available. Look them up in your phone book or check out their websites: www.redcross.org.uk and www.sja.org.uk.

When to call 999

If your child is seriously hurt, is unconscious or you think he may have suffered a spinal injury you should always call an ambulance. The same applies if your child needs emergency treatment and you don't have any suitable transport to take him to hospital yourself, or you're unsure of how to get to your nearest A & E department.

Although paramedics are the best people to deal with a medical emergency, time is of the essence in these situations and it's often quicker to take your child to your nearest hospital yourself than to wait for an ambulance to arrive. Of course, you should only do this if your child can be moved safely.

When you call for an ambulance the operator will want to know your name and that of your child as well as the exact location of the emergency. You'll be asked what has happened and how your child has been affected. Try to remain calm so that you can give the operator as much information as possible. It's important to stay on the line until the operator tells you to hang up as he or she will be able to help you deal with the emergency until the ambulance arrives.

Treatment at home

Minor cuts and grazes

Most minor cuts and grazes can be treated at home unless you are concerned about infection, in which case you'll need to take your child to your doctor's surgery.

What you should do

1 Clean the wound and surrounding area under a running tap and then use an antiseptic cream or solution to reduce the risk of infection.

2 Cover with a plaster or a dressing once the surrounding area is dry.

Bites and stings

Bites from mosquitoes and midges and stings from wasps and bees can be very painful and itchy. Rarely, people have an allergic reaction to wasp and bee stings so if your child has difficulty breathing as a result of a sting you should call 999 immediately. In normal circumstances a bite or sting can be treated at home.

What you should do

1 If the sting has been left in the skin remove it with tweezers, taking care not to squeeze the poison sac as this would force more poison into the skin.

2 Apply a cold cloth or pack of frozen peas wrapped in a towel to the area to relieve the pain.

3 Once your child is more comfortable massage sting-relief cream into the area.

A cold cloth applied to the area which has been stung or bruised will help reduce any swelling.

Bruises and swelling

This is usually caused by a fall or bump which leads to discoloration and swelling in the affected area. It normally disappears within a week.

What you should do

1 Hold a cold cloth or a pack of frozen peas wrapped in a towel to the area for about 30 minutes. This will help to reduce the swelling.

Breathing problems

Choking

If your baby gets something lodged in his throat he will turn blue and make gasping noises. If you can't remove the obstruction yourself you will need to call an ambulance.

What you should do

1 Lay your baby face down with his chest and abdomen lying along your forearm. Support his head with your hand. Alternatively lay him across your knee with his head facing down.

2 Give him five sharp slaps in the middle of his back, checking between each slap to see if the obstruction has cleared.

3 If this fails, turn him face up and use your finger to try to remove the blockage, making sure that you don't push it further down his throat.

4 If you can't feel anything and your child is still choking, put two fingers on the lower half of his breastbone and press down sharply five times.

5 If the blockage is still there, dial 999 and keep on repeating steps 2 and 4 until the blockage is removed or the ambulance arrives.

6 If your child becomes unconscious you may need to give rescue breaths or CPR (*see* right).

Unconscious baby

What you should do

1 If your baby is unconscious, check to see if he is breathing by looking for chest or tummy movement. If he's breathing, call an ambulance.

2 While you're waiting for it to arrive hold him against you with his head lower than his chest so that his airway is open. Keep checking his pulse and breathing until the ambulance arrives.

3 If your child is unconscious and has stopped breathing you will need to start giving rescue breaths at once and continue until breathing resumes. If possible get someone else to call the ambulance, but if you have to do this yourself keep your baby with you.

Rescue breaths

What you should do

1 Make sure the airway is open by keeping your baby's head back with one hand on his forehead and a finger under his chin.

2 Take a deep breath and then place your lips over your baby's mouth and nose, making sure that the seal is airtight.

3 Blow steadily until you see your baby's chest rise, then take your lips away and watch the chest fall.

4 Give two rescue breaths and check for signs of circulation.

Checking circulation

What you should do

1 Use your index and middle fingers to feel for a pulse on the inside of the upper arm.

2 If a pulse is present continue giving rescue breaths at a rate of eight every one minute until your child starts breathing on his own or the ambulance arrives. If there is no pulse you should start upon Cardiopulmonary Resuscitation (CPR) immediately.

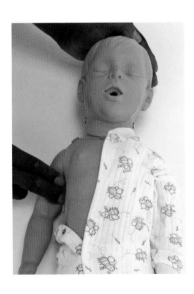

Cardiopulmonary resuscitation (CPR)

What you should do

1 Imagine a line drawn between your baby's nipples and then place the first two fingers of one hand a finger-width below this line in the middle of his chest.

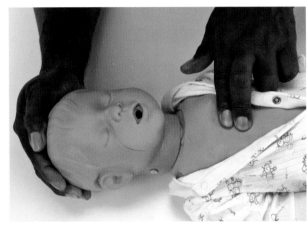

2 Using the tips of these two fingers, press down firmly so that the chest is depressed by about 2.5 cm (1 in). Repeat rapidly five times.

3 After five compressions give a rescue breath (*see* left).

4 Continue giving five compressions followed by a rescue breath (aiming for a rate of about 100 compressions a minute) until the ambulance arrives.

Injuries requiring medical help

Serious wounds

A wound that is deep and bleeding heavily will need immediate treatment to control the blood flow. Once the bleeding has been stemmed your child will need to see the doctor or go to the A & E department at a hospital.

What you should do

1 If the cut is on an arm or leg, raise the limb and support it while applying pressure to the wound, using an absorbent sterile dressing if possible.

2 Cover the wound with a sterile dressing, bandage firmly to help keep the bleeding under control and get medical help.

Burns and scalds

Burns are caused by dry heat such as flames or hot electrical equipment. Scalds result from wet heat such as steam or water that's too hot. There is a risk of infection from both, so you should always seek medical advice.

1 Cool the damaged area of skin under cold running water for at least ten minutes.

2 Remove anything that may constrict the area if it swells, but don't attempt to remove any material such as clothing that is sticking to a burn.

3 Cover with a sterile dressing or cling film and take your child to the doctor's surgery.

Broken bones

A broken or cracked bone is known as a fracture and should be treated with great care because any undue movement could lead to further damage. Your child will need to be taken to the hospital.

What you should do

1 Keep your child still and warm.

2 Remove anything which could restrict swelling around the injured area.

3 Get urgent medical help.

Eye injuries

Immediate first aid treatment will be needed if your child injures an eye and you'll need to take him to the hospital.

What you should do

1 If there is a foreign object in the eye use a damp piece of cotton wool to remove it. If this fails, or the eye remains painful, cover it with a clean pad before taking your child to the hospital.

2 If the injury was caused by a blow, apply a sterile dressing and go to the hospital.

3 Chemicals splashed into the eye need to be washed out by flooding the eye with clean water for at least 15 minutes. The eye should then be covered and your child taken to the hospital.

Dialling 112

It's worth knowing that in the case of an emergency you can also contact the emergency services by calling 112 from anywhere within the EU, including the UK from a fixed or mobile phone.

Useful addresses

Newborn
Premature babies
BLISS
9 Holyrood Street
London SE1 2EL
Helpline freephone: 0500 618140
www.bliss.org.uk

Doulas
Doula UK
PO Box 26678
London N14 4WB
Tel: 0871 433 3103
www.doula.org.uk

Maternity Nurses
The Maternity Nurse Company
London House
100 King's Road
London SWQ6 4LX
Tel: 0845 257 8400
www.maternitynurse.co.uk

Week 1
Breastfeeding
The Association of Breastfeeding
Mothers
PO Box 207
Bridgwater
Somerset TA6 7YT
Helpline: 0870 401 7711
www.abm.me.uk

National Childbirth Trust
Alexandra House
Oldham Terrace
London W3 6NH
Helpline: 0870 444 8708
www.nct.org.uk

La Leche League
PO Box 29
West Bridgford
Nottingham NG2 7NP

Helpline: 0845 120 2918
www.laleche.org.uk

Week 2
Maternity and paternity rights
www.dti.gov.uk

Bottle feeding
www.babyfriendly.org.uk
www.nhsdirect.nhs.uk/articles/
article.aspx?articleId=641
www.hebs.scot.nhs.uk/readysteadybaby
/youandyourbaby/bottlefeeding.htm

Safe sleeping
Foundation for the Study of
Infant Deaths (FSID)
Artillery House
11–19 Artillery Row
London SWP 1RT
Helpline: 020 7233 2090
www.sids.org.uk

Week 3
Nappies
Women's Environmental Network
PO Box 30626
London E1 1TZ
Tel: 020 7481 9004
www.wen.org.uk/nappies

Tommee Tippee
Careline @ Jackel International Ltd
Dudley Lane
Cramlington
Northumberland NE23 7RH
Careline: 0500 97 98 99
www.tommeetippee.co.uk

National Association of Nappy
Services
Tel: 0121 693 4949
www.changeanappy.co.uk

Week 4
Crying
BM Cry-sis
London WC1N 3XX
Helpline: 0845 1228 669
www.cry-sis.org.uk

Week 6
Support for Dads
Home Dad
Tel: 0775 254 9085
www.homedad.org.uk

Week 7
Health information
www.thefamilygp.com

NHS Direct
Tel: 0845 46 47
www.nhsdirect.nhs.uk

Forehead thermometer
Bosieboo
Suite C
St Nicholas Close
Fleet
Hants GU51 4JA
Tel: 0800 180 4225
www.bosieboo.com

Week 8
Immunisation
www.immunisation.nhs.uk

Postnatal depression
Association for Post-natal Illness
145 Dawes Road
London SW6 7EB
Helpline: 020 7386 0868
www.apni.org

Week 11
Benefits
www.hmrc.gov.uk

Play
National Association of Toy and
Leisure Libraries
www.natll.org.uk

England:
68 Churchway
London NW1 1LT
Tel: 020 7255 4604

Scotland:
First Floor, Gilmerton Community Centre
4 Drum Street
Edinburgh EH17 8QG
Tel: 0131 664 2746

Wales:
Steeple House
Steeple Lane
Brecon
Powys LD3 7DJ
Tel: 01874 622097

Week 13
Health Visitors
www.healthvisitors.com

Week 14
Childcare
SureStart
2nd Floor, 188-190 Earls Court Road
London SW5 9QG
Helpline: 0845 767 8111
www.childcareapprovalscheme.co.uk

National Childminding Association
Royal Court
81 Tweedy Road
Bromley BR1 1TG
Tel: 0845 880 0044
www.ncma.org.uk

Childcare Link
Freephone: 08000 960 296
www.childcarelink.gov.uk

Direct Gov
www.direct.gov.uk

Ofsted
Royal Exchange Buildings
St Ann's Square
Manchester M2 7LA
Tel: 08456 404040
www.ofsted.gov.uk

Week 15
Second-hand goods
The Baby Products Association
2 Carrera House
Merlin Court
Gatehouse Close
Aylesbury HP19 8DP
Helpline: 0845 456 9570
www.b-p-a.org

Week 16
Passport Service
Advice line: 0870 521 0410
www.passport.gov.uk/index.asp

European Health Insurance card
www.dh.gov.uk/traveller

Sun safety
www.sunsmart.org.uk

Week 17
Grandparents
The Grandparents' Association
Moot House
The Stow
Harlow
Essex CM20 3AG
Helpline: 01279 444964
www.grandparents-association.org.uk

Week 19
Help and Advice
Citizens Advice Bureau
www.adviceguide.org.uk

Books for babies
Bookstart
www.bookstart.co.uk.

Week 21
Swimming
Immunisation and swimming
www.immunisation.org.uk

Swim nappies
www.splashabout.net

Special baby wetsuits
18 Oregon Avenue
Tilehurst
Reading
Berks RG31 6R2
Tel: 0845 365 3645
www.incywincy.net

Week 22
Financial advice
Association of Independent Financial
Advisors
Austin Friars House
2–6 Austin Friars
London EC2 2HD
Tel: 020 7628 1287
www.aifa.net

Wills
The Law Society
Tel: 020 7242 1222
www.lawsociety.org.uk

Week 23
Lone parents
One Parent Families
255 Kentish Town Road
London NW5 2LX
Helpline: 0800 018 5026
www.oneparentfamilies.org.uk

Gingerbread
Advice line: 0800 018 4318
www.gingerbread.org.uk

Dads UK
www.dads-uk.co.uk

Domestic Violence
Mankind
Helpline: 0870 794 4124
www.mankind.org.uk

Women's Aid Federation of England
PO Box 391
Bristol BS99 7WS
Helpline: 0808 2000 247
www.womensaid.org.uk

Week 24
Safety
Royal Society for the Prevention of
Accidents
RoSPA House
Edgbaston Park
353 Bristol Road
Edgbaston
Birmingham B5 7ST
Tel: 0121 248 2000
www.rospa.com

Kid Rapt Ltd
56 Barton Road
Luton
Beds LU23 2BB
Tel: 01582 493382
www.childsafety.co.uk

Child Accident Prevention Trust
4th Floor, Cloister Court
22–26 Farringdon Lane
London EC1R 3AJ
Tel: 020 7608 3828
www.capt.org.uk

Week 25
Weaning
www.eatwell.gov.uk

Week 26
Allergies
Asthma UK
Summit House
70 Wilson Street
London EC2 2DB
Helpline: 0845 7010 203
www.asthma.org.uk

Asthma UK Scotland
4 Queen Street
Edinburgh EH2 1JE
Tel: 0131 226 2544

Asthma UK Cymru
3rd Floor
Eastgate House
34–43 Newport Road
Cardiff CF24 0AB
Tel: 02920 435 400

Asthma UK Northern Ireland
Peace House
224 Lisburn Road
Belfast BT9 6GE
Tel: 02890 669736

National Eczema Society
Hill House
Highgate Hill
London N19 5NA
Helpline: 0870 241 3604
www.eczema.org

Galactosaemia
Galactosaemia Support Group
31 Cotysmore Road
Sutton Coldfield
West Midlands B75 6BJ
Tel: 0121 378 5143
www.galactosaemia.org

First Aid
British Red Cross
44 Moorfields
London EC2Y 9AL
Tel: 0870 170 7000
www.redcross.org.uk

St John Ambulance
Tel: 08700 10 49 50
www.sja.org.uk

NHS Direct
Tel: 0845 46 47
www.nhsdirect.nhs.uk

Scotland: NHS24
Tel: 08454 24 24 24
www.nhs24.com

Index

Acknowledgements

First and foremost, my thanks have to go to Dr Peter Wilkinson MBChB, MRCGP, DCH, DRCOG for all the help and advice he gave me while writing the book, and to my dear friend and health visitor extraordinaire, Jane Batt, who was on the end of the phone whenever I needed her. Thanks also to all the mums with their wonderful babies who not only agreed to be photographed for this book but were also happy to share their concerns, thoughts and feelings about early motherhood with me. Special thanks, too, to photographers Maree Lock and Ben Cowlin for taking such wonderful pictures and for making the photo shoots so enjoyable. I'm also very grateful to my friends Tina and Pat for their help at home which gave me hours more writing time, and to my editor Laura Kesner at HarperCollins for her unfailingly good-natured support and enthusiasm for the project. Finally, and most importantly, none of this would have been possible without my three wonderful children, Dominic, Lucy and Kate, who gave me the experience on which this book is based.

Picture credits

All photography by Maree Lock except for the following:

pp.10, 11, 19, 25, 26, 30, 38-9, 40, 44, 45, 46, 52, 56, 58, 60, 73, 77 left, 78, 98, 102, 103, 129, 137, 143, 151, 152, 156, 160 Ben Cowlin; pp.12, 55 Mother & Baby Picture Library/Eddie Lawrence; p.13 Joe Bator/Corbis; pp.15, 20, 21, 97, 107, 108, 141, 159, 162 Getty Images; p.24 Sally Inch/Mark-It TV; pp.50, 111 Mediscan; p.66 Pulse Picture Library; p.109 Jennie Woodcock, Reflections Photolibrary/Corbis; p.126 Ome Design, pp.132-33, 163 Bubbles; p.165 Jean-René and Constanze Dedieu; pp.167, 168, 169 Book Creation.